An American Icon

Very few companies have the privilege of tracing their roots to an American icon. *Gaylord Entertainment Company* is honored to call the world-famous WSM Grand Ole Opry its cornerstone. What began 75 years ago in 1925 as a simple radio broadcast formed the foundation for a company that today produces entertainment across the country and around the world.

Though Gaylord Entertainment Company is widely recognized for its entertainment, our greatest source of pride are the Friday and Saturday night Opry shows that originate from Nashville every weekend. Each Opry broadcast is as special and unique as the many members and guests artists who give of themselves and their talents week after week to create a show that not only entertains a live audience of thousands but reaches out to radio listeners everywhere.

The Grand Ole Opry is unique in that no other musical genre has a home like country music has at the Opry. And, in addition to being country music's most legendary and historical show, in simple terms, the Grand Ole Opry is home to its members. And, to those members, the Opry is very much a family. It is funny stories shared in the hallway as well as supporting others when the going gets tough—just like family members do.

The Opry is also inspiring—not only to fellow performers but to those who tune in or attend each week. That inspiration travels many miles from the Opry stage across the airwaves. In its 75-year history, everyone from Roy Acuff and Minnie Pearl to Porter Wagoner and Loretta Lynn to Vince Gill and Patty Loveless has listened and wanted to become a part of it. These artists and many others have become Opry members and have ensured that this revered institution continues to thrive.

Gaylord Entertainment Company is inspired in much the same fashion. We honor the Grand Ole Opry as it celebrates its 75th anniversary. As we mark this milestone, we also look to our next 75 years as the caretakers of our company's crown jewel.

Official Opry® Picture-History Book

Editors/Writers: Dan Rogers, Jerry Strobel, Trish McGee, Judy Mizell
Photographers: Ruth Bauer, Donnie Beauchamp, Jeb Dekalb, Jerry Gaza, Jim Hagans, Russ Harrington (Connie Smith), Larry Hill, Gary Layda, Les Leverett, Eddie Malone, Alan Mayor, Judy Mock, Theresa Montgomery, Hope Powell (Billy Walker), Jim McGuire (Riders in the Sky)
Interior Layout/Design: Ellen Parker Bibb
Cover Design: Gina R. Binkley, Altar Ego Design
Copyright: 2000 Gaylord Entertainment Company; Nashville, Tennessee; Volume 11, Edition 1; Price $10

TABLE OF CONTENTS

Bill Anderson

There's an old saying "If you want someone's attention, whisper." That is more than just an old saying when you are referring to Bill Anderson. That's a fact!

His soft way of breathing a country song earned him the name "Whispering Bill" at the start of his career. Along the way he earned some other names such as multi-million-selling recording artist, award-winning songwriter, actor, television show host, and author.

Bill was born in Columbia, South Carolina, but grew up around Atlanta, Georgia, working his way through the University of Georgia as a disc jockey. While he studied, he sang and wrote songs, such as Ray Price's country classic "City Lights" when he was only 19. Bill earned a journalism degree, then moved to Nashville where he began a string of hits that hasn't stopped yet.

He has had 72 singles of his own on the charts and hundreds of songs that were hits for other artists. He has released 50 albums and won more than 50 BMI songwriting awards—more than any other writer in the history of country music. He was elected to the Nashville Songwriters Association Hall of Fame and the Georgia Music Hall of Fame.

He was voted Songwriter of the Year six times, Male Vocalist of the Year, received Duet of the Year with two different singing partners—Jan Howard and Mary Lou Turner—wrote the Song of the Year and twice recorded the Record of the Year.

An avid sports fan, he was watching the All Star baseball game on television when he got the call inviting him to join the Grand Ole Opry. He became a member on July 15, 1961.

His list of hits includes some of the best known country songs—"Tips of My Fingers," "When Two Worlds Collide," "Po' Folks," "Where Have All the Heroes Gone," "Still the One," "I May Never Get to Heaven," "Once a Day" and his monster single "Still."

He has written and co-written hits for Brenda Lee, Jim Reeves, Dean Martin, Roger Miller, Debbie Reynolds, Roy Clark, Connie Smith, Ivory Joe Hunter, Faron Young, Eddy Arnold, Jean Shepard, Aretha Franklin, Conway Twitty, Lawrence Welk, Roy Acuff and Jerry Lee Lewis. Wade Hayes, Vince Gill, Steve Wariner, Lorrie Morgan, Mark Wills and Tracy Byrd have recorded Bill's songs, too.

He was the first country artist to host a network game show—ABC's *The Better Sex*—and he appeared on ABC's *One Life to Live* for three years. He hosted numerous TNN shows, including the game show *Fandango*. These days, you can often find him hosting TNN's *Opry Backstage*.

His 1989 autobiography, *Whisperin' Bill*, is in its fourth printing, and his latest work, the hilarious *I Hope You're Living As High On the Hog As the Pig You Turned Out to Be*, was published in 1993.

Today, he still writes, records, and performs across the country. His 1998 album *Fine Wine* was produced by fellow Opry member Steve Wariner.

And the hits just keep coming. Bill had two No. 1 records in 1999—Mark Wills "Wish You Were Here" and "Two Teardrops" by Steve Wariner.

Bill welcomes Mark Wills, who enjoyed a No. 1 hit with Bill's "Wish You Were Here," to the Opry stage.

Ernie Ashworth

It is a long way from
the cotton fields of
Alabama to the
Grand Ole Opry, but
. . . "It's a lot more fun
than the cotton field."

Ernie Ashworth was at the Redstone Arsenal in his hometown of Huntsville, Alabama, when his records started shooting up the charts like the guided missiles he was working on. With his sights set on a country music career, he headed back to Music City.

Ernie, who was playing and singing on Huntsville radio station WBHP by the time he was 20, had great success in Nashville as a songwriter in the early '50s. Signed as an exclusive writer for Acuff-Rose, Nashville's first music publishing company, he wrote hits for such country greats as Little Jimmy Dickens, Carl Smith, Johnny Horton and Wilma Lee Cooper. Even pop star Paul Anka recorded one of his songs, "I Wish."

Ernie Ashworth first hit Nashville as a songwriter.

But success as a recording artist evaded him, and he went back to Huntsville. In 1960 Wesley Rose called him to record again. His second try at making it as a singer was indeed the charm.

His first record, *Each Moment* went Top 10 nationally. So did his second, *You Can't Pick a Rose in December.*

In 1963 came the smash hit he had been waiting for. "Talk Back Trembling Lips" went to No. 1 and stayed on the national charts for 36 weeks. It also did well on the pop charts, making it one of the first crossover records. It also inspired another big hit for Ernie—his stage suit with the big red lips outlined in gold studs. It has become his signature, and the audiences love it.

In 1963 and 1964, he was voted Most Promising Male Artist by *Cashbox, Billboard* and *Record World* magazines. And on March 7, 1964, Ernie saw his lifelong dream come true when he was invited to join the Grand Ole Opry.

Ernie gave the movie business a try in 1965, appearing in *The Farmer's Other Daughter.*

He received the Living Legend Award from the Major Independent Record Label Awards Show in 1991, and that same year Curb Records released an album of original recordings collected from his Top 10 hits. In 1992 Ernie was inducted into the Alabama Music Hall of Fame.

In 1999, Ernie celebrated 35 years as an Opry member with a new hit single. "Lonely's Only Bar" was the No.1 independent recording on OnlineCountry's Tracker Weekly Country Chart and the song was No.1 on the Most Played Independents in Europe. "She Don't Drink, She Don't Smoke But She Lies" was another successful single for him.

Ernie still plays road dates and recently completed a European tour. He still brings the house down with his hits and trembling lips suit, but he is also a businessman. In 1989 he bought radio station WSLV in Ardmore, Tennessee, just 20 miles from Huntsville, Alabama.

It is a long way from the cotton fields of Alabama to the world-famous stage of the Grand Ole Opry. But as Ernie is fond of saying, "It's a lot more fun than the cotton field."

Clint Black

When Clint Black burst onto the music charts in February 1989 with the song "Better Man," the first of five consecutive No. 1 hits from his debut album *Killin' Time*, he became the first artist ever to have five No. 1 singles on a debut album.

On April 22, 1989, Clint first appeared on the Opry. While singing "Killin' Time," he remembers "feeling" Opry legends Hank Williams and Ernest Tubb. After leaving the stage, he learned that he had stood on a circular piece of wood from the historic Ryman stage that is now a part of the Opry stage. Clint got goose bumps just thinking about it.

Clint Black joined the Opry in 1991, the same year he took CMA Male Vocalist of the Year honors.

In October of 1989, the goose bumps continued for Clint when he accepted the Country Music Association's (CMA) prestigious Horizon Award on stage during a live telecast from the Grand Ole Opry House. Clint said, "It was like stepping into a picture that I had been looking at all of my life."

Clint returned to that stage on January 10, 1991, when he was inducted as an Opry member during the taping of the *Opry's 65th Anniversary Special* on CBS-TV. Referring to his earlier comment at the awards show, he said, "The picture keeps getting better and better."

That picture has only improved for Clint in the years since. He has established a sterling reputation as a singer, songwriter, producer and actor.

The former Houston honky-tonker has scored more than 25 Top 10 hits including "Nobody's Home," "Loving Blind," "Like the Rain," "Nothing's News" and "Something That We Do." He has co-written songs with Merle Haggard, Jimmy Buffett, Marty Stuart and Don Henley.

His debut album went triple platinum and each successive release has been a million seller including *Killin' Time, Put Yourself in My Shoes, The Hard Way, No Time to Kill, One Emotion, Nothin' But the Taillights.*

In 1998, Clint earned rave reviews for his role in the television film *Still Holding On: The Jack Favor Story*. In 1999's *Going Home*, he appeared opposite Jason Robards Jr.

Clint won the CMA's Male Vocalist of the Year Award, the American Music Award for Favorite New Male Country Artist and received Album, Single, Best Male and Best New Male Vocalist awards from the Academy of Country Music—all in one year, 1990.

His humanitarian efforts were recognized on March 2, 2000, when the Country Radio Broadcasters presented Clint with the Humanitarian of the Year Award.

In 1999, he released *D'Lectrified*, his own salute to the songs and musicians who had a big impact on his development as a musician. It also features the No. 1 duet "When I Said I Do," a collaboration with his wife, actress Lisa Hartman Black. The song won the couple the ACM's Vocal Event Award in 2000.

Garth Brooks

Garth Brooks considers his Opry membership the pinnacle of his entertainment career. That's quite a statement coming from an artist who has won almost every major award and sold millions of records.

The youngest of six children, Garth was born in Tulsa, Oklahoma, but grew up in Yukon, an oil town near Oklahoma City. He first moved to Nashville in 1985, but returned home after just 23 hours. After completing a degree in advertising at Oklahoma State University, he returned to Music City in 1987. Within six months, he had signed a recording contract with Capitol Records.

Garth's first single, "Much Too Young (To Feel This Damn Old)," from his self-titled debut album made it to No. 8 on the charts. Three No. 1 hits followed— "Not Counting You," "The Dance" and "If Tomorrow Never Comes," making *Garth Brooks* the biggest selling album of the 1980s.

What followed was a career that far exceeds the Oklahoman's wildest expectations.

Having sold more than 99 million records, Garth is the top-selling solo artist of the century, according to the Recording Industry Association of America. He is also the only male artist to have four albums—*No Fences*, *Ropin' the Wind, The Hits* and *Double Live*— to each exceed sales of 10 million.

Garth has received nearly every accolade the recording industry can bestow upon an artist, including two Grammys, 16 American Music, 11 Country Music Association, 18 Academy of Country Music, five World Music, 10 People's Choice and 24 *Billboard* Music Awards. Both the American Music Awards and the Academy of Country Music Awards named him Artist of the Decade in 1999. He also has a star on the legendary Hollywood Walk of Fame.

Garth's television credits include eight NBC specials, a guest appearance on *Empty Nest* and *Muppets Tonight!* as well as a cameo appearance on NBC's *Mad About You*. He also has hosted *Saturday Night Live*. His film production company, Red Strokes Entertainment, is based in Los Angeles.

Garth Live from Central Park in 1997 drew the largest concert crowd to New York's Central Park. The HBO special was the most-watched cable television special that year.

Still, his induction into the Grand Ole Opry on October 6, 1990, remains one of the highest honors for this singer/songwriter.

"To be recognized as a member of the Opry is among the class of honors that will never be topped no matter how long or how far my career goes," Garth said.

A typical Garth Brooks Opry visit: fans, photos and autographs backstage.

Jim Ed Brown

SOME OF JIM ED'S

EARLIEST MEMORIES ARE

OF CLOSE, FAMILY TIMES

WHEN THEY WOULD ALL

GATHER AROUND THE

BATTERY-POWERED

RADIO TO LISTEN TO

THE GRAND OLE OPRY

ON SATURDAY NIGHT.

Not many singers top the charts as a member of a trio, duet, and as a solo artist. But then there aren't many like Jim Ed Brown.

The Sparkman, Arkansas, native was one of five children—two boys and three girls—of a struggling lumberman and his wife. Some of Jim Ed's earliest memories are of close, family times when they would all gather around the battery-powered radio to listen to the Grand Ole Opry on Saturday night.

Jim Ed and his older sister Maxine, fascinated by what they heard, began harmonizing together and soon were appearing on local radio while he was still in high school.

By his second year in college, Jim Ed and Maxine were regulars on the Little Rock KLRA "Barnyard Frolic" and soon wrote their first hit, "Looking Back To See."

They became members of the Louisiana Hayride and joined Red Foley as featured regulars on his Ozark Jubilee in 1955.

Later that year, younger sister Bonnie joined them, and they became the Browns, scoring an instant Top 10 hit with "Here Today and Gone Tomorrow." The group signed with RCA in 1956 and followed with two No. 1 songs—"I Take the Chance" and "I Heard the Bluebird Sing."

After a two-year stint in the service, Jim Ed joined his sisters again and in 1959 they hit with the big one. "The Three Bells" sold more than a million copies and was the first No. 1 country song to cross over and hit No. 1 on the pop and rhythm and blues charts. They followed with hits "The Old Lamplighter" and "Scarlet Ribbons."

The Browns joined the Opry on August 12, 1963. But by the mid-'60s, both Bonnie and Maxine decided that combining busy careers and caring for growing families was too much and they retired.

Jim Ed went solo and continued the success. In 1966 he scored with one of the great beer drinking songs—"Pop a Top"—which went to No. 3 on the charts.

The '60s and '70s saw more hits— "Southern Loving," "Sometime Sunshine" and "Morning."

In 1975 he began a six-season run as co-host of the syndicated weekly television series Nashville on the Road, and he became the national advertising spokesperson for Dollar General Stores.

Then in 1976 he teamed with Helen Cornelius for one of country's most successful duets. They released hit after hit—"Don't Bother To Knock," "Fools," and the No. 1 releases "I Don't Want To Have to Marry You," "Saying Hello, Saying I Love You, Saying Goodbye," "You Don't Bring Me Flowers" and "Lying in Love with You."

In 1983, Jim Ed became host of TNN's You Can Be a Star, the country music talent search which aired daily on The Nashville Network. In 1994 he paired with his wife Becky as co-hosts of TNN's travel show Going Our Way.

Today he is still the smooth-voiced crowd pleaser every time he takes center stage. Sometimes the crowd gets to witness a real Opry magical moment—when Maxine and Bonnie reunite with Jim Ed on stage and once again the Browns are together in the spotlight.

Jim Ed, Maxine and Bonnie Brown ("The Browns") harmonize on one of the biggest group hits in country music history, "The Three Bells."

Bill Carlisle

When it comes to country comedy and novelty songs you could say Bill Carlisle wrote the book. He has been performing and recording the best and funniest hits for 60 years.

Bill has written hundreds of songs—so many that as he once told a writer, "People used to come up to the stage and mention songs even I had forgotten about."

But if he has forgotten them he is the only person who ever forgot a Bill Carlisle song. Who could forget such records as "Too Old to Cut the Mustard," "What Kinda Deal Is This?," "Knothole," and "Is Zat You, Myrtle."

Friends Bryan White and Jimmy Dickens help Bill celebrate another birthday in the Opry's Green Room.

"WHEN I WAS GROWING

UP OUR FAMILY'D GET

TOGETHER FOR A GOOD

OLD-FASHIONED SING-ALONG

EVERY SUNDAY. . . MOM,

DAD, MY FOUR BROTHERS,

TWO SISTERS AND ME."

"When I was growing up, our family'd get together for a good old-fashioned sing-along every Sunday," he recalls. "We had quite a chorus with mom, dad, my four brothers, two sisters and me. Those were great days back in Wakefield, Kentucky. I'm sure they had a lot to do with my becoming a musician and entertainer."

In the '30s Bill and his older brother Cliff were popular stage and radio entertainers, and Bill had a hit single "Rattlesnake Daddy" in the '40s. But it was a giant hit called "Rainbow at Midnight" in 1946 that put the Carlisles in the country music spotlight.

"Knoxville was the country music center in the early '50s," explains the broad-grinning Bill, "so we packed up our show and moved from Ohio to Tennessee." The Carlisles played with such famed performers as

Don Gibson, Chet Atkins, the Carter Family, Homer and Jethro, Carl Butler and Archie Campbell. In November 1953, Bill and his group joined the Grand Ole Opry.

Every performer has a certain style on stage, and so does Bill. He jumps! "I just do it, always have," he says. The jumping dates back to the early 1950s when he was performing with brother Cliff, an accomplished singer and steel and dobro player. They were performing on the "Midday Merry-Go-Round" on radio station WNOX in Knoxville. To add comedy to the act, brother Bill dressed up as "Hotshot Elmer," a character he had created in the 1940s. Staging a mock fight and placing a chair between the two brothers, a barefooted Elmer could stand flat-footed and jump over the chair . . . and jump back. The jumping drew so many laughs that he incorporated this into the act.

Country fans loved his crazy humor—in his songs and on stage. "Too Old to Cut the Mustard" was in the Top 10 in 1952, and "No Help Wanted" went to No. 1.

Today the Carlisles consist of his son Bill Jr., George Riddle and Joe Edwards.

In 1993 Bill suffered a heart attack and underwent quadruple bypass surgery—which curtailed his jumping. However, he was soon back performing on the Opry. Even hip surgery in 1994 hasn't kept "Jumpin' Bill" from entertaining the Opry audience with his comedy and humor. You never know what he will come up with—but you know it will be wild and the audience will be laughing.

One thing's for sure, Bill Carlisle will never be "Too Old to Cut the Mustard."

Roy Clark

When country music first crossed over onto the pop charts, Roy Clark was there. When a small town in the Ozarks became known as the live music capital of the world, it was Roy who started it. When the longest-running syndicated television series in history was on the air, it was Roy Clark who starred in it.

It surprises people to learn that this self-described "hillbilly singer" and Meherrin, Virginia, native was raised in Washington, D.C. where his father, who played in a square dance band, took him to free concerts given by the National Symphony and military bands. His dad taught him the banjo. (Roy is a virtuoso of all stringed instruments and also plays trombone, trumpet and piano.)

He got his first guitar, a Sears Silvertone, for Christmas at age 14, the same year he made his first television appearance. He began playing D.C. bars and dives at night and skipping school—eventually dropping out at 15.

The guitar wizard was soon touring with country legends Grandpa Jones and Hank Williams. Winning a national banjo competition in 1950 also won him an invitation to play the Opry. That led to shows with Red Foley and Ernest Tubb. In between he would return to D.C. to play jazz, pop and early rock 'n' roll—even backing Elvis.

At 27, Roy was still scrambling, but an invitation to open for Wanda Jackson was his big break. It led to his own tour—365 straight nights—and a trip to Vegas as a headliner. The next year he had his first hit, "The Tips of My Fingers," a country song with an orchestra and strings.

The '60s were filled with concerts, hits, and TV variety shows from *Mike Douglas* to *Flip Wilson* to *The Tonight Show*. Then came *Hee Haw,* which premiered in 1969, co-starring Roy and Buck Owens. It was an immediate hit and still in the Top 20 when CBS canceled the show after only two-and-a-half years. That didn't stop the cornfield capers. It ran in syndication until 1992.

Since 1969 Roy has won 25 major awards including the Country Music Association's Entertainer and Instrumentalist of the Year honors and Instrumental Group of the Year (with Buck Trent). His Academy of Country Music achievements include Comedy Act, Lead Guitar and Entertainer of the Year and the Pioneer Award. He has a star on Hollywood's Walk of Fame and a Grammy for "Alabama Jubilee" (1982).

He became a member of the Grand Ole Opry on August 22, 1987.

His long list of hits features "Yesterday When I Was Young," "I Never Picked Cotton," "Thank God and Greyhound You're Gone," "Somewhere Between Love and Tomorrow" and "Come Live With Me."

In 1983, he created another first when he opened the Roy Clark Celebrity Theatre in Branson, Missouri, and started the Branson live theatre phenomenon.

Roy lives in Tulsa, Oklahoma. A look at his concert schedule tells you that live performances are what it is all about for Roy. His calendar is filled with shows in theaters, resorts, and the big casinos of Vegas.

Roy's philanthropic generosity is legend. He has donated nearly one million dollars to the Children's Medical Center of Tulsa. A new section of St. Jude's Children's Hospital in Memphis is named after Roy. He has raised more than one million dollars for the facility.

Roy Clark is in his element...live on the Opry Stage.

John Conlee

John Conlee's string of No. 1 hits certainly didn't get him off the farm. It gave him the chance to get back to it and live a way of life he loves.

"I spend all of my off-time, what I have of it, with my family on our farm," he explains. "I enjoy it. There's no glamour to it. Woodworking, gunsmithing or driving a tractor require getting grease or varnish all over you. It's dirty work, but I like it."

"There are more of us ordinary folks than anybody else," says the singer of the everyday, middle class life in his hits "Common Man," "Working Man" and "Friday Night Blues."

John grew up on a 250-acre farm in Kentucky where he raised hogs, cultivated tobacco with mules and mowed pastures. He also worked as a funeral home attendant and mortician, and as a pop music disc jockey in Nashville before settling into a career in country music in the mid 1970s.

In 1976 John signed with ABC/Dot Records and released "Backside of Thirty." This and two more singles earned him some support but not success.

In 1978, "Rose Colored Glasses," a song he co-wrote with Glenn Barber that would become his signature song, took off. He followed it with "Lady Lay Down" which went to No. 1.

The next year he re-issued "Backside of Thirty" and it went to No. 1. The hits "Before My Time" and "Baby, You're Something" came next and in 1979 he

was named the Academy of Country Music's Best New Male Vocalist.

The hits kept coming—"Friday Night Blues," "She Can't Say That Anymore," "Miss Emily's Picture," "Busted" and "I Don't Remember Loving You."

On February 7, 1981, John became a member of the Grand Ole Opry.

In 1983 and 1984 John scored four consecutive No. 1 hits—"Common Man," "I'm Only in it for the Love," "In My Eyes" and "As Long as I'm Rockin' with You." His *John Conlee's Greatest Hits* was named one of the top country albums, and he was voted No. 5 on the list of overall top artists of 1983-84 by *Billboard* magazine.

Other Top 10 hits followed—"Way Back," "Years After You," "Working Man," "Old School," "Harmony," "The Carpenter" and "Domestic Life."

In 1986 "Got My Heart Set on You" went to No. 1, and he released the album *Fellow Travelers* in 1989.

Always the banner carrier for the common man, John was instrumental in the crusade for America's farmers that became the Family Farm Defense Fund. He helped Willie Nelson, Neil Young and John Mellencamp organize and entertain at the Farm Aid concerts that raised more than $13 million in grants for farmers.

He also is deeply involved with the "Feed the Children" charity and has raised more than $140,000—one dollar at a time—from the dollar bills tossed on the stage when he sings his 1982 hit "Busted."

John maintains an active touring schedule and recently released the album *Live at Billy Bob's Texas.*

Two distinct voices meet on the Opry stage: John Conlee and Patti Page.

JOHN HAS RAISED MORE THAN $140,000 FOR THE "FEED THE CHILDREN" CHARITY FROM THE DOLLAR BILLS TOSSED ON THE STAGE WHEN HE SINGS HIS HIT "BUSTED."

Wilma Lee Cooper

"I SING JUST LIKE I DID

BACK WHEN I WAS

GROWING UP IN THOSE

WEST VIRGINIA

MOUNTAINS. I COULDN'T

SING ANY OTHER WAY."

Wilma Lee Cooper is officially the first and foremost woman in bluegrass and traditional mountain music.

In 1974 the Smithsonian Institution, Washington, D.C., honored her as "First Lady of Bluegrass Music" at an institution-sponsored folk festival. Today many of her songs are preserved in the Smithsonian's Archives of the Performing Arts Division as well as the Library of Congress Archive of American Folk Music and Harvard University's Library of Music.

Wilma Lee is a rarity in a practically all-male form of music. Also rare and unique is her powerful, clear and true singing voice—backed by her big D-45 Martin guitar, the fiddle, five string banjo, dobro guitar and bass.

Born Wilma Leigh Leary, she grew up in the wild and beautiful mountains of West Virginia. Her family was a well-known music group the "Leary Family" who performed at bluegrass and folk festivals.

About the same time she got her degree in banking from Davis and Elkins College, she met and married another traditional performer Dale. T. Cooper and as Wilma Lee & Stoney Cooper, the pair created a team that was to make an important place in the history of country music. Two skillful musicians and songwriters as well as singers, they recorded such classics as "Tramp on the Street," "Walking My Lord Up Calvary's Hill" and "The Legend of the Dogwood Tree" for Columbia.

They continued their success on the Hickory label with "Come Walk With Me," "Big Midnight Special" and "There's a Big Wheel."

"I sing just like I did back when I was growing up in those West Virginia mountains. I've never changed. I can't change. I couldn't sing any other way," Wilma Lee says. "I would say my style is just the old mountain style of singing. I am traditional country. I'm a country singer with the mountain whang to it."

She notes that she sings a lot of story songs, and if listeners don't understand the words to that type of song they miss the story. "So, when I sing, I try to speak my words as plainly as I can, so folks will know what I am saying."

Following Stoney's death on March 22, 1977, Wilma Lee assembled a talented group of young musicians, the Clinch Mountain Clan, and they continued to perform. She is intensely proud of their character and integrity as well as their musicianship and never fails to introduce them on the Opry by name, adding emphatically, "I'm proud of every one of 'em."

Today she still brings traditional music to the Opry stage, often performing with her daughter Carol Lee who leads the Carol Lee Singers—the four-member group that provides background vocals for Opry performers.

Both the Smithsonian and her fans everywhere have proclaimed her one of the great singers of the traditional mountain music. Her songs—sad, happy and plaintive—seem to take listeners back to the rugged slopes, clean mountain air and lush meadows of West Virginia.

Friends and musical collaborators: Wilma Lee and buddy Marty Stuart celebrate a successful Opry performance of "Pretty Polly."

Skeeter Davis

It's a far cry—and quite a few miles— from Dry Ridge, Kentucky, to the stage of the Grand Ole Opry, but Skeeter Davis successfully spanned the distance when she joined the Opry cast on August 4, 1959.

And she didn't stop there. For more than 43 years Skeeter has circled the globe, performing everywhere from New York City's Carnegie Hall and London's Royal Albert Hall to concert halls and theaters throughout the world. She has sung in every major city in every state (except Alaska) as well as in England, Germany, Japan, Holland, Sweden, Norway, Ireland, Denmark, Finland, New Zealand, the Virgin Islands, Singapore, Malaysia, Korea and Jamaica where she is extremely popular.

She has performed in small clubs and large theaters, at fairs and rodeos, at music festivals and on radio and television. She has done shows with everyone from Eddy Arnold and Ernest Tubb to Connie Francis, Bobby Vinton, the Beach Boys, the Righteous Brothers, the Rolling Stones, Aretha Franklin, Gladys Knight & the Pips, the Grateful Dead and Elvis Presley.

Throughout her successful musical career, she remained faithful to the Opry which she listened to growing up in Kentucky. The first born of seven children of William and Sarah Penick, little Mary Frances was nicknamed Skeeter by her grandfather because she was always "skeeting here and there" like a water bug. The name stuck.

Skeeter had entertained her brothers and sisters at an early age but didn't take singing seriously until she met Betty Jack Davis in high school in Covington, Kentucky. They started performing together, billing themselves as the Davis Sisters. Winning a talent contest got them a spot on a local television station. This led to other radio and television

appearances and ultimately a recording contract with RCA Victor in 1952.

The following year their first single "I Forgot More (Than You'll Ever Know)" went to No. 1, sold a million copies and became a gold standard. Then tragedy struck on Aug. 2, 1953. As they were returning home after performing on the WWVA Wheeling Jamboree, their car was hit head-on by another car whose driver had fallen asleep. Betty Jack was killed and Skeeter was injured seriously—both physically and emotionally.

As she would do many times in her life, Skeeter overcame that tragedy. She recorded and toured briefly with Betty Jack's sister Georgia before pursuing a solo career in 1958. With Chet Atkins as her producer, Skeeter found success in the form of Top 10 hits, gold records, numerous awards and honors for her singing and songwriting including Most Promising Female Vocalist. She also received five Grammy nominations, including one for her first Top 10 hit "Set Him Free" in 1959.

More success came in 1963 when "The End of the World" became the very first No. 1 country/pop crossover and a Top 10 hit worldwide. Other big hits followed with "Gonna Get Along Without You Now," "Bus Fare To Kentucky" and "One Tin Soldier."

Bus Fare To Kentucky also is the title of Skeeter's 1993 autobiography. The book is a testimony to Skeeter's strong faith in God. In it she recounts the joys and sorrows in her life—such as her bout with cancer in 1988. For all who know her, Skeeter is a shining example of the power of courage and religious faith. Skeeter continues to perform regularly on the Grand Ole Opry, stepping into the Opry spotlight and entertaining fans just as she has done since joining the Opry cast more than 40 years ago.

Backstage greetings: Skeeter checks in with Opry guest Brad Paisley.

Diamond Rio

As one entertainment writer noted, Diamond Rio has the kind of problem any singing group would love to have—too many hits to fit into one show.

With their lighter-than-air harmonies and intricately woven instrumentation, this six-man group has been transforming great songs into standards since the release of its self-titled 1991 debut album.

Since then, the band has been awarded Vocal Group of the Year honors 12 times collectively from the Country Music Association and the Academy of Country Music while garnering seven Grammy nominations. Diamond Rio has sold more than five million records, including six No. 1 singles and 15 Top 5 hits.

Diamond Rio features the talents of Marty Roe (lead vocals), Gene Johnson (mandolin, harmony vocals), Jimmy Olander (lead guitar), Brian Prout (drums), Dan Truman (keyboards) and Dana Williams (bass guitar, harmony vocals).

Diamond Rio evolved from the Tennessee River Boys, a band that Marty, Jimmy and Dan worked in at the Opryland themepark before leaving in 1986 to form their own group. Brian and Gene joined in 1987, Dana in 1989. In 1991, the group's debut single "Meet in the Middle" went to No. 1. It was followed by two Top 5 hits that same year—"Mirror, Mirror" and "Mama Don't Forget to Pray for Me."

The group attributes Diamond Rio's success to its keen ability to choose just the right songs with that personal touch. The success is evident in the No. 1 songs "Norma Jean Riley," "In a Week or Two," "Love a Little Stronger," "Walkin' Away" and "How Your Love Makes Me Feel." The group's other hits include "That's What I Get for Loving You," "Holdin'," "You're Gone" and "Unbelievable."

Diamond Rio made its first Opry appearance on October 4, 1991. On April 18, 1998, Diamond Rio became the first group (since the Whites in 1984) to be inducted into the Opry.

"You can't compare this to the other awards. It's wonderful to be recognized by the industry, but I rank the Opry right up there with the Hall of Fame. We put this right at the top of the heap," said Marty Roe of their Opry membership.

For Dana Williams, Opry membership was special because his uncles—better known as bluegrass legends the Osborne Brothers—have been Opry members since 1964.

The group hosts the annual Diamond Rio Charity Golf Tournament which has raised more than $200,000 for the American Lung Association. The band also serves as national celebrity spokesperson for the national Big Brother/Big Sister organization.

The Opry's first inducted group since The Whites, Diamond Rio gets together backstage. Left to right: Dana, Jimmy, Marty, Gene, Dan and Brian.

Jimmy Dickens

Though he stands just 4 feet 11 inches tall, Little Jimmy Dickens is a giant among country entertainers. Just ask his fellow Opry members, who call him "the littlest but the biggest star at the Opry." It has been that way since 1948 when Jimmy hit the Opry stage wowing the audience with flamboyant rhinestone-studded outfits, wild novelty hits and country humor.

Jimmy was the oldest of 13 children born to a West Virginia farmer. Even as a child, Jimmy knew he wanted to perform. He started singing on local radio station WOLS in Beckley, West Virginia, while he was in college at the University of West Virginia, opening the station's program "crowing like a rooster." Even though Jimmy had to walk to and from the station, he set his sights on an entertainment career. And he hasn't looked back.

After winning local acclaim, he moved on to WIBC in Indianapolis and then to Cincinnati's WLW.

It was Roy Acuff who introduced Jimmy to the Opry in 1948, and soon he joined the ranks of Hank Williams (who nicknamed him "Tater"), Lefty Frizzell and Eddy Arnold by releasing hit after hit on Columbia Records. Songs like "A-Sleepin' at the Foot of the Bed," "Take an Old Cold Tater," "Little, but I'm Loud," "Out Behind the Barn," "Country Boy," "Wabash Cannonball" and dozens of others.

"Proud members of the Friends of Tater Club:" David Gates and Billy Dean talk with the Hall of Famer before making an Opry guest appearance.

Jimmy became a regular on the popular TV show *Stars of the Grand Ole Opry* which was shown around the world. He appeared on the *Phillip Morris* TV Show for 18 months before resigning to entertain abroad—13 trips to Europe, three to Southeast Asia and twice to Vietnam where he entertained troops under fire.

In the spring of 1964 Jimmy became the first country music artist to completely circle the globe on a world tour. That same year he broke into the pop music spotlight with his recording of "May the Bird of Paradise Fly up Your Nose." It topped the country charts and went to No. 15 on the pop charts, and Jimmy found himself on all of the network shows. He continued with such hits as "We Could," "Life Turned Her That Way," "Raggedy Ann" and "Preacher Man."

In 1983, the Country Music Association recognized Jimmy and his stellar career achievements by inducting him into the Country Music Hall of Fame during its annual awards show.

In 1989 the Reunion of Professional Entertainers gave him a Golden ROPE Award and Rounder Records released his 1949-55 hits on an album titled *Straight From the Heart.*

In 1996, Jimmy and his wife Mona celebrated 25 years of wedded bliss by renewing their wedding vows on the Opry stage. When he is not working, they enjoy the quiet life at their Brentwood home south of Nashville.

In recent years Jimmy has appeared on CMT and TNN as a frequent guest in Vince Gill's music videos. Although he retired from touring, he still brings the house down every weekend at the Opry.

Joe Diffie

Joe Diffie has earned a reputation as a singer's singer, a master song craftsman and a flawless judge of great country lyrics.

Joe grew up in a musical family. His dad played guitar, and his mom sang. Early musical influences came from riding in the family pickup singing "You Are My Sunshine" and listening to his dad's great record collection of George Jones, Merle Haggard, Johnny Cash and Lefty Frizzell.

This former Oklahoma iron foundry worker moved to Music City in 1986. His bluegrass and country roots ran deep, and his "quick study" abilities rapidly attracted attention in the songwriting and publishing community.

In between shifts at the Gibson Guitar warehouse, Joe sang demos on "I've Cried My Last Tear for You" (which would later become a hit for Ricky Van Shelton), "Born Country" (likewise for Alabama) and "You Don't Count the Cost" (Billy Dean).

Joe's compositions were recorded by Charley Pride, Hank Thompson, the Forrester Sisters, Tracy Lawrence and Doug Stone, just to name a few. Holly Dunn topped the charts in 1989 with "There Goes My Heart Again," a song he co-wrote.

Joe landed his recording contract with Epic Records in 1990. In just one year, he placed five songs at the top of the charts— "If You Want Me To," "New Way to Light up an Old Flame," "Home," "If the Devil Danced in Empty Pockets" and "Ships That Don't Come In."

The Tulsa, Oklahoma, native finished his debut year by being named *Cash Box* magazine's Male Vocalist of the Year and *Billboard* magazine's Top Singles Artist of the Year.

His first two albums—*A Thousand Winding Roads* and *Regular Joe*—achieved gold status. *Regular Joe* also produced the Top 10 hits "Is It Cold in Here," which he wrote, and "Startin' Over Blues." *Honky Tonk Attitude* in 1993 yielded the hits "Prop Me Up Beside The Jukebox" and "John Deere Green." That same year, he won a Country Music Association award for his collaboration with George Jones on "I Don't Need Your Rocking Chair."

Joe became an Opry member on November 27, 1993.

In 1994, he released *Third Rock From the Sun* followed by *Life's So Funny* (1995) and *Twice Upon a Time* (1997). After his *Greatest Hits* collection in 1998, he won a Grammy in 1999 for his performance on "Same Old Train," a Marty Stuart song from the *Tribute to Tradition* album. His latest release, *A Night to Remember*, features four songs that he wrote as well as the title track, another Top 10 hit.

THIS FORMER OKLAHOMA IRON FOUNDRY WORKER MOVED TO MUSIC CITY IN 1986—AND RAPIDLY ATTRACTED ATTENTION. . .

On March 11, 2000, Joe Diffie wed Theresa Crump in the conservatory gardens of the Opryland Hotel.

Roy Drusky

Roy Drusky's mom, a church organist for 20 years, couldn't get him interested in musical training—and she tried. He was too interested in baseball. "I ate, slept and breathed baseball," he says. But while his mother couldn't get him interested in piano practice, singing was different. Besides, the Young People's Choir at the Moreland Baptist Church allowed him time to play baseball.

Roy bought his first guitar while he was in the Navy. After an unsuccessful tryout for the Cleveland Indians, he formed a band. He performed regularly over WEAS in Decatur, Georgia, and became a disc jockey. Soon, he added two weekly television shows in Atlanta. Roy was doing live shows in the area when Minneapolis Radio Station KEVE made an offer.

"My time in Minneapolis proved to be both pleasant and invaluable," says Roy. "I didn't realize what devoted country fans those people were in the upper Midwest. I got a boost to my career and my ego during my 18-month stay."

He made several trips to Nashville during his Minneapolis stint and when Faron Young had a smash hit with his "Alone With You," Roy knew he had to take advantage of his success and move to Music City.

He became a member of the Opry on June 13, 1958.

The '60s were good to Roy. He released "Another," "Alone With You," and a duet with Kitty Wells, "I Can't Tell My Heart That." In 1965 he teamed up with Priscilla Mitchell to record "Yes, Mr. Peters" which became his first No. 1 hit.

Numerous Top 10 hits followed— "I'd Rather Loan You Out," "I Went Out of My Way," "Three Hearts in a Tangle," "Second Hand Rose," "Peel Me A Nanner," "(From Now On All My Friends Are Gonna Be) Strangers," "Such A Fool" and "All My Hard Times."

His hit single "White Lightning Express" was from the movie by the same name, a film that added acting to Roy's credits. He also made two other country and western films, *Forty Acre Feud* and *Golden Guitar*.

When he wasn't acting or singing, he was producing other artists and directing the office of SESAC, a music licensing firm he helped establish.

Today, Roy's focus is on recording country/southern gospel albums. He has five to his credit on the Chapel/Bridge label, and he performs gospel concerts nationwide with Evangelist Kenneth Cox.

Roy Drusky offers the Opry audience one of his signature ballads.

Holly Dunn

Holly Dunn began her career as a hit songwriter, penning chart-toppers for a host of country stars. She moved from behind the scenes to center stage in the mid-'80s with a string of 10 consecutive Top 10 songs.

Holly was born and raised in San Antonio, Texas, the youngest of four children and daughter of a Church of Christ minister. Her brother Chris moved to Nashville and began a successful career in songwriting when she was a sophomore. As soon as Holly earned her degree in public relations and advertising from Abilene Christian University, she, too, was on her way to Music City.

"I saw what Chris was doing and thought, 'Hmmm...I grew up in the same house as he did. I played guitar just like he did, and I'd been writing songs since I was a kid and performing them all the time," she recalls. She wanted to try her hand at music in Nashville.

Within a year she landed a staff songwriter deal with a major Nashville publisher. Four years later she moved to the newly formed MTM Records, a label in search of an artist who was also a songwriter. The label found that perfect combination in Holly. She launched her singing career in 1986 with "Daddy's Hands," originally recorded by the Whites but written by Holly as a Father's Day Gift in 1985. Holly's version in 1986 stayed in the Top 10 for six months and earned her two Grammy nominations.

Over the next three years she recorded three top-selling albums for MTM. When MTM folded in 1989 she changed labels, going to Warner Brothers where her hot streak continued. Her debut album produced the No. 1 hit "Are You Ever

Gonna to Love Me." Other No. 1 songs followed—"Love Someone Like Me," "Only When I Love" and "You Really Had Me Going."

She was named the Academy of Country Music's Top New Female Vocalist in 1986 and received the Country Music Association's Horizon Award in 1987. She garnered Grammy nominations and won the 1987 Nashville Songwriters Association's International Award for "Daddy's Hands." In addition, she took home the 1988 BMI Country Songwriter of the Year award.

Holly's Opry invitation came in 1989. She had learned to love the Opry seeing the Opry stars on tour in San Antonio when she was a tiny tot of 2 and 3 and had made numerous guest appearances before becoming an official member on October 14, 1989.

In 1992, Holly took a break from recording and stayed out of the studio for three years. The creative vacation paid off. She recorded *Life and Love and All the Stages*, writing all but one song on the album—that one she left to brother Chris.

Her latest album, *Leave One Bridge Standing*, reunited her with producers and hit-writers Don Cook, the man behind the sound of superstars Brooks & Dunn, and Chris.

Today, Holly is back in Nashville after spending 1997 as co-host of the morning show at Detroit's powerhouse country station WWWW. There she became the first country recording artist to have a major market radio show.

Two CMA Horizon Award winners hook up backstage during a Jo Dee Messina visit to the Opry. "Country music to me is the Opry. And the Opry is country music," Holly says.

The Gatlin Brothers

"WE DIDN'T EXACTLY

HAVE YOUR NORMAL

CHILDHOOD, BUT WE

DID HAVE OURSELVES A

HECK OF A LOT OF FUN

WITH THE MUSIC."

The Gatlin Brothers began singing together as a baby gospel group in their home state of Texas. They won their first talent contest in 1954 at a Hardin-Simmons University talent show in Abilene when Larry was 6, Steve 4, and Rudy was only 2.

Their father was an oil driller who had to move from job to job, town to town, taking his family with him—eight different towns in one year alone. Through their travels their music and religion were a mainstay, and after finally settling in Odessa, it was the gospel groups like the Blackwood Brothers and the Statesmen who drew the Gatlin family to their shows.

After high school the Gatlin boys went in different directions, and it was a while before they would sing together again.

While attending the University of Houston on a scholarship, Larry heard that gospel group The Imperials would be backing Elvis Presley in Las Vegas, and they needed a baritone. He auditioned but didn't get the job—not this time anyway.

Larry played football at the University of Houston and flirted with the idea of becoming a lawyer. Steve and Rudy graduated from Texas Tech, and both became teachers. But, their hearts were in their music.

In the meantime, Larry was on a month long gig singing in Vegas with the Imperials and Jimmy Dean. Also on the bill was Dottie West, who would become his mentor and friend.

"Dottie offered to help me," Larry recalls. "She said I looked enough like Mickey Newbury that maybe I could write a song. I sent her eight songs and a month later she sent me an airplane ticket to Nashville. This was in May 1971."

Dottie recorded two of those songs—"Once You Were Mine" and "You're The Other Half of Me." She also played Larry's tape for Kris Kristofferson and Fred Foster at Monument Records. Soon the Gatlin siblings, including sister LaDonna, left Texas for Tennessee.

In 1974 Monument Records signed Larry, and the Gatlins were soon working with Tammy Wynette. But, the Gatlin Brothers wanted to perform their music together. So Larry wrote a song especially for the three—it took 15 minutes, he recalls. The song was "Broken Lady." It went to No. 1 and won the Gatlins a Grammy in 1976.

They joined the Grand Ole Opry on Christmas Day 1976.

"All the Gold in California" climbed the charts in 1979. In the next 10 years they had 18 Top 20 hits, including "Houston (Means I'm One Day Closer to You)" and "Night Time Magic."

In the early '90s Larry earned great reviews for his work in the Broadway musical "The Will Rogers Follies."

During that time, the brothers scaled back their touring and recording schedule to concentrate on their theater in Myrtle Beach, South Carolina, where they have performed as many as 30 weeks a year

Most recently Larry starred in the Broadway touring production of "The Civil War." Steve performed in "Summer of '66," a musical revue in Myrtle Beach. Rudy—a scratch golfer—spends his time improving his golf game.

Larry maintains a strong touring schedule and released his autobiography *All the Gold in California: and Other People, Places & Things* in 1998.

Steve, Larry and Rudy are at home on stage or the golf course.

Don Gibson

Music Row first wanted him as a songwriter. He wanted to perform. So, Don Gibson wrote enough hits for himself and everybody else.

For starters, "I Can't Stop Loving You," "Oh, Lonesome Me," "(I'd Be) A Legend in My Time" and "Sweet Dreams." Don's songs have been recorded by more than 150 artists—from Elvis Presley to Elvis Costello and Ferlin Husky to Ella Fitzgerald.

Born in Shelby, North Carolina, Don was the son of a railroad man. With three brothers and two sisters, Don knew early on that he would be responsible for financing his music career. So, he went to work in the textile mills and "hopping curbs and even delivering baby diapers," he recalls, just to earn enough money.

A songwriting legend, Don Gibson penned "I Can't Stop Loving You" and "Oh, Lonesome Me" in the same afternoon.

DON WENT TO WORK IN

THE TEXTILE MILLS AND

"HOPPING CURBS AND

EVEN DELIVERING BABY

DIAPERS," HE RECALLS,

JUST TO EARN ENOUGH

MONEY TO FINANCE HIS

MUSIC CAREER.

Don was only a kid when he moved to Knoxville, Tennessee, to be a regular on the WNOX "Tennessee Barndance." He also played area club dates and one-nighters.

Wesley Rose, president of Acuff-Rose Publishing in Nashville, saw Don perform. Wesley's father Fred Rose had discovered Hank Williams. Wesley Rose offered Don a songwriting contract. But, since Don wanted to sing, he told Wesley that it was a deal only if he got to perform. So, his writing contract was with Wesley, his recording contract with RCA.

His first single "Too Soon to Know" became a known song, but it was the second one that garnered the attention—

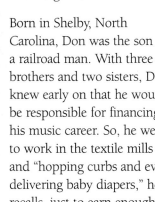

"Oh, Lonesome Me." He wrote it in the same afternoon that he wrote "I Can't Stop Loving You." But Don didn't think much of "Oh, Lonesome Me."

"I thought it was nothing at all, so I sent it to Nashville and said, 'Give it to George Jones. It might make him a good number,'" he remembers. "I had no idea I'd ever cut it."

"But Chet Atkins and Wesley Rose said that was the one they wanted me to record. I said, 'I don't want to do that junk. I thought you'd give it to George.' Well, they insisted, so I said 'I'll do it if you let me put "I Can't Stop Loving You" on the back. I think it's the best song.' Chet and Wesley reluctantly agreed to use the song, and "I Can't Stop Loving You" became a country standard in spite of them."

Don further justified his talents with such hits as "Blue Blue Day," "Legend In My Time," "Sweet Dreams," "Too Soon To Know," "Guess Away The Blues, "Country Green," "Who Cares" and scores of others. So many that you can't separate Don Gibson the singer from the songwriter.

Don joined the Opry on May 20, 1958. But according to Don the nicest thing to happen to him in his career is his wife Bobbie—a beautiful charmer from his hometown of Shelby.

So, what is Don's musical goal after more than 40 years as a legend? "To top myself. I'd like to write another hit as big or bigger than "I Can't Stop Loving You," and I think I can do it, too." That's a safe bet.

In the meantime Don's fans can load up on his hits from recent collections *A Legend in My Time, Oh, Lonesome Me* and *Collector's Series.*

Vince Gill

As one of country music's most accomplished singers, songwriters and musicians, Vince Gill is truly regarded as a triple threat.

The Oklahoma native's first instruments were a four-string tenor guitar and his dad's banjo. He soon made a name for himself playing in bluegrass bands throughout his high school years.

After moving to Los Angeles, Vince worked as a sideman in such bands as the Bluegrass Alliance and Byron Berline's Sundance. He became the lead singer of Pure Prairie League in 1979, performing its hits "Let Me Love You Tonight" and "Still Right Here in my Heart." He later worked in the Cherry Bombs, backing Rodney Crowell and Rosanne Cash.

Vince moved to Nashville in 1984 and landed his first recording contract. However, the next five years found him busy doing studio work on other artists' projects or touring with Emmylou Harris.

He joined the MCA Records roster in 1989 and scored his first No. 1 on the country charts with "When I Call Your Name," a song he co-wrote. A string of hits followed including "Liza Jane," "Don't Let Our Love Start Slippin' Away," "One More Last Chance," "What the Cowgirls Do," "A Little More Love," "Never Knew Lonely," "I Still Believe in You," "When Love Finds You," "Pretty Little Adriana," "Go Rest High on That Mountain" and "If You Ever Have Forever in Mind."

He joined the Opry on August 10, 1991.

Vince has won more Country Music Association awards than any other artist in history, having claimed 18 since 1990 when he took home Song of the Year honors for "When I Call Your Name."

At the 42nd Annual Grammy Awards, he surpassed his good friend Chet Atkins for the most Grammy Awards won by a country artist with 14. Vince is the only country artist to win a Grammy 11 consecutive years. In all, he has claimed more than 70 industry awards recognizing his work as a vocalist, songwriter and guitarist. His career record sales exceed 21 million.

In his spare time, Vince maintains a one handicap on the golf course. He hosts "The Vinny," his annual Pro-Celebrity Invitational tournament that benefits the Tennessee Junior Golf program.

Vince's humanitarian efforts on behalf of countless charities have been recognized with the Minnie Pearl and Harmony Awards in 1993. He was named Tennessean of Year by the Tennessee Sports Hall of Fame in 1994.

On March 10, 2000, Vince married contemporary Christian/pop singer Amy Grant.

Vince shares a laugh with Opry buddies Porter Wagoner and Patty Loveless.

Billy Grammer

. . .MUSIC WAS A BIG

PART OF FAMILY LIFE

AND BILLY OFTEN

PLAYED FIDDLE, GUITAR

OR MANDOLIN FOR

FAMILY GATHERINGS AND

AT LOCAL EVENTS.

Billy Grammer, the singer, is also one of the great guitar players of country music. One of the finest flat-top guitars on the market —the Grammer Guitar—is named for him.

Billy was born one of 13 children to a coal mining family in Benton, Illinois, and spent his childhood on a farm fishing the Wabash River and dreaming of becoming a mechanical engineer.

But music was a big part of family life and Billy often played fiddle, guitar or mandolin for family gatherings and at local events. "Daddy played the fiddle—or violin if you like—and we entertained at the social functions around home," Billy remembers. "We were poor, but everybody else, was too. I had one good pair of bib overalls which I scrubbed on the old rub board myself."

After high school he served in the Army and spent an apprenticeship as a toolmaker. After the war he found himself like thousands of other soldiers—without work.

Billy got word of a possible opening with Connie B. Gay, a disc jockey with WARL radio in Arlington, Virginia. Gay was promoting Grand Ole Opry acts in that three-state area and Billy hitchhiked to Arlington, auditioned, and got the job.

As a great musician, he began performing in the bands of other artists like Hawkshaw Hawkins and Grandpa Jones. He was also a sideman on the Jimmy Dean television show. He formed his own band and began performing as a solo artist. In early 1959 he recorded his hit "Gotta Travel On," and on February 27, 1959, he became a cast member of the Grand Ole Opry.

A superb instrumentalist, Billy was always in great demand as a session picker. "I've got a little more of a broad sense of music than the average guy coming up playing country music," the 40-year Opry member says. "Musicians I have talked to through the years have told me that I have a little extra punch, a little extra push. They said it was enough to make them sit up and start listening but not so much that they'd stop listening."

With this exceptional guitar style, Billy recorded the albums *Gospel Guitar, Country Guitar* and *Sunday Guitar.*

Billy soon turned his talents to developing what has been called "the finest flat-top guitar on the market"—the Grammer Guitar. The first instrument came off the production line in 1965 and was donated to the Grand Ole Opry Museum.

In 1990 he was inducted into the Illinois Country Music Hall of Fame—along with Tex Williams, Lula Belle & Scotty, and Patsy Montana.

Billy and his wife of 55 years, Ruth, live in Illinois but he still performs often on the Opry.

The Opry audience goes to "Grammer school" as Billy again masters his instrument of choice.

Jack Greene

BORN AND RAISED IN THE

FOOTHILLS OF THE GREAT

SMOKY MOUNTAINS,

JACK LEARNED TO PLAY

GUITAR AT AGE 8 AND

AS A TEENAGER HAD HIS

FIRST RADIO JOB.

For Jack Greene 1967 was "a really good year." His hit "There Goes My Everything" held the No. 1 position on the national charts for seven weeks, went to No. 2 for two weeks and back to No. 1 for another two weeks. The album topped the charts for a year.

In the fall of 1967 he took the Country Music Association's awards for Single of the Year, Album of the Year, Song of the Year and Male Vocalist of the Year.

Jack joined the Opry on December 23, 1967.

It was one of the most fantastic years ever experienced by a country artist and just the beginning of a fantastic career for the guy nicknamed the "Jolly Green Giant" who started as a drummer and singer with Ernest Tubb and his Texas Troubadours.

Born and raised in the foothills of the Great Smoky Mountains, Jack learned to play guitar at age 8 and as a teenager had his first radio job. At age 18 he was appearing on the "Tennessee Barn Dance" on WNOX in Knoxville, Tennessee. From there he moved to Atlanta working with the Cherokee Trio, the Rhythm Ranch Boys and Cecil Griffith & the Young 'Uns.

Following a stint in the Army he was back in Atlanta and for the next 10 years performed throughout the south with the Peachtree Cowboys.

In 1962 he joined Ernest Tubb's Texas Troubadours and began performing regularly on the Opry. Two years later Dottie West asked him to sing the male part on "Love Is No Excuse," a song she had recorded with Jim Reeves shortly before his death. Thanks to Dottie and Ernest he got to be in the spotlight enough to venture out on his own in 1967.

He followed his phenomenal first hit with eight more No. 1 songs—"All The Time," "What Locks The Door," "You Are My Treasure," "Until My Dreams Come True," "Back in the Arms of Love," "Love Takes Care of Me," "Lord, Is That Me?" and "Statue of a Fool." He also had two No. 1 albums and a hit single with Jeannie Seely who joined his road show and recorded with him for several years.

In 1989 he was inducted into the Atlanta Country Music Hall of Fame.

That same year he thrilled fans at the Superstar Spectacular show during Fan Fair when he joined Ricky Van Shelton for a duet of "Statue Of A Fool," a hit for Jack in 1969 and for Ricky 21 years later.

"Music is my life and it's important for me to please my audiences," Jack says seriously. "Nothing can take the place of those special feelings when you have played your best and the audience realizes this and shows their approval. I perform my music for me and for the people. If I can continue doing this, I am happy."

Today he continues to make fans happy with his Opry appearances.

"Hmmm . . ." Jack rehearses before a stirring delivery of "The Lord's Prayer."

Tom T. Hall

Kurt Vonnegut, a close literary colleague of Tom T. Hall, describes Tom T. as a "flying fish" because he is good at more than one thing. In the country music world, Tom T. is often referred to simply as a legend.

Singer, songwriter and author, Tom T. was born and raised in Olive Hill, Kentucky, the fourth son of a brick plant worker and ordained Baptist minister. Tom T. began playing guitar at age 4 and wrote his first song at 9. In his teens, he formed a bluegrass band, and the group performed at a local radio station until its members were drafted into the Korean conflict.

Tom T. stayed at the station as a disc jockey, but later joined the Army in 1957. Afterwards he moved to Roanoke, Virginia, to work as a radio copywriter. It was in Roanoke that Tom T. would write songs which were recorded by Johnny Wright, Jimmy C. Newman, Dave Dudley, Bobby Bare and Burl Ives.

In 1964 he moved to Nashville where for the next five years, he wrote songs eight hours a day, five days a week. He soon started recording the songs he had written, the first for Mercury Records in 1968 entitled "I Washed My Face in the Morning Dew" which became a Top 10 hit.

His second, "A Week in a County Jail," went to No. 1.

But, it was the next song, recorded by Jeannie C. Riley, that became an international country and pop hit—"Harper Valley PTA." It sold six million records and won the Country Music Association's Single of the Year Award and the 1968 Grammy for Song of the Year.

In January 1971, Tom T. joined the Grand Ole Opry.

A member of the Songwriters Hall of Fame, his songs have been recorded by Perry Como, George Jones, Loretta Lynn, Johnny Cash, Dolly Parton, Willie Nelson, Waylon Jennings, George Burns and Patti Page. In 1996, Alan Jackson topped the charts with "Little Bitty," a song written by Tom T.

While he had firmly established himself as a songwriter, Tom T. continued his own recording career with such hits as "Old Dogs, Children and Watermelon Wine," "The Year Clayton Delaney Died," "I Love," "Ravishing Ruby," "I Like Beer" and numerous others.

In all, Tom T. has recorded 45 albums, won more than 50 BMI Awards, a Grammy and garnered seven CMA nominations.

Also an accomplished author, Tom T. has written seven books including an autobiography, a songwriting textbook, a collection of short stories and two novels.

Tom T. and his wife Dixie, also a successful songwriter, live in Tennessee and Florida and are deeply involved in songwriting and the recording and production of acoustic music.

It's alright to be Little Bitty, and it's alright to have your song cut by Alan Jackson. Two Opry members get together in Nashville to celebrate the success of "Little Bitty."

George Hamilton IV

Travel is a way of life for George Hamilton IV. One look at his passport confirms that. Certainly, no one would dispute his unofficial title as the "International Ambassador of Country Music."

"We're on, by George!" The IV and V wait for their cue to hit the Opry stage.

Along with his title, George IV has compiled an impressive list of firsts. He appeared at the first "International Festival of Country Music" in London (1969) and performed at the first such international festivals in Sweden (1976), Finland (1977), Holland and Norway (1978), Germany (1979), Paris and Zurich (1980) and Vienna, Austria (1984).

He was the first American country singer to appear in Russia and Czechoslovakia (1974) and the first American to record a studio album in Eastern Europe (Prague, 1982).

George IV was the first American country singer to have his own British TV series. He also appeared in England's first Country Music Summer Season show.

The "firsts" don't end here. George IV also was the first pop artist to switch to country music. As a college student, he gained stardom with the 1956 million-selling Top 10 pop hit "A Rose and a Baby Ruth" and spent weekends and vacations touring.

One evening in 1960, sitting in the Ryman Auditorium enjoying the Opry, George IV decided to switch from pop to country music. After all, his roots were in country.

At age 12 or 13, this North Carolina native saved his paper route money and, with his parents' permission, rode a bus to Nashville to see the Opry. From his room,

George IV watched Red Foley and Ernest Tubb go into the National Life building to rehearse. Going over to watch rehearsals, he met Chet Atkins who invited him to go backstage at the Opry that night.

After George IV moved to Nashville to pursue a country music career, Chet signed him to RCA Victor. In March 1960 George IV joined the Grand Ole Opry. That same year he had his first country hit, "Before This Day Ends."

In 1963 "Abilene" was his first No. 1. Other major hits included "Fort Worth, Dallas, or Houston," "Truck Driving Man," "Early Morning Rain," "She's A Little Bit Country" and "Break My Mind."

Several of his hits were written by Canadian artist Gordon Lightfoot whose work he admired. George IV worked extensively in Canada, even hosting a TV series in that country for six years. His other TV credits include starring in his own show on ABC in 1959.

From Canada, George IV ventured to Europe, New Zealand, South Africa, Hong Kong, Australia and the Holy Land where he videotaped two TV specials with Arthur Smith.

He took a break from the Opry in 1971 to move back to North Carolina to spend time with his family and devote time to television work in Canada and Great Britain. He moved back to Nashville in 1976 and plays the Opry regularly when he's not off to Europe and points beyond.

GEORGE'S FAVORITE SONG IS "LIFE'S RAILWAY TO HEAVEN."—"THAT WAS MY GRANDFATHER'S FAVORITE SONG," HE SAYS. "HE WAS A RAILROAD MAN AND HE TAUGHT ME TO LOVE COUNTRY MUSIC."

Emmylou Harris

Award-winning Emmylou has multiple Grammys to her credit.

Few artists have a musical background as diverse as Emmylou Harris. And, few artists have had the profound effect on contemporary music that she has had.

Born in Birmingham, Alabama, to a military family, Emmylou spent her childhood in North Carolina and graduated valedictorian from high school in Woodbridge, Virginia.

After winning a dramatic scholarship to the University of North Carolina she began to seriously study music— especially the songs of folk singers Bob Dylan and Joan Baez. She sang in a local college folk duo and left school for the Greenwich Village New York scene to try her luck at a professional music career. She played the clubs, sharing the stage with legends like Jerry Jeff Walker and David Bromberg.

Emmylou began to draw attention on the club circuit in both New York and D.C. and in time was introduced to her mentor Gram Parsons, formerly of the Flying Burrito Brothers and a heralded pioneer in the burgeoning country-rock movement. Emmylou toured and recorded with Gram until his tragic death in 1973.

"After he was gone I wanted to carry on with what I thought he would have wanted me to do," she recalls, "bringing certain elements of folk music, with its emphasis on the lyric, trying electric things, but always coming back to that electric country base."

In 1975 she recorded her first album *Pieces of the Sky* introducing her Hot Band which over the years has known such world-class players as Albert Lee, Rodney Crowell, Ricky Skaggs and Hank DeVito.

Her best-selling albums include *Elite Hotel, Luxury Liner, Quarter Moon in a Ten-Cent Town, Blue Kentucky Girl, Roses in the Snow, Evangeline, Cimmaron, Bluebird, Angel Band, Cowgirl's Prayer, Wrecking Ball* and *Light of the Stable.*

Emmylou has enjoyed seven No. 1 hits and 27 Top 10 songs including "If I Could Only Win Your Love," "Together Again," "Sweet Dreams," "Making Believe," "To Daddy" and "Heartbreak Hill."

She has eight gold albums and eight Grammy Awards, including one for her 1987 *Trio* album with Linda Ronstadt and Dolly Parton. In 1999, Linda, Dolly and Emmylou reunited for *Trio II*, and won a Grammy for Best Country Collaboration. Also, she and Linda recorded *Western Wall: The Tucson Sessions* the same year.

In addition to her own albums she has sung on albums with many other performers — including Bonnie Raitt, Willie Nelson, Ricky Skaggs, Vince Gill, Trisha Yearwood, Lyle Lovett, the Judds, and Garth Brooks.

In 1999, *Billboard* magazine recognized her distinguished career achievements with its highest accolade—the Century Award.

On January 25, 1992, she was inducted into the Grand Ole Opry and summed up her feelings about her music: "Music is like food, sustenance. You certainly don't do it for the spotlight . . .You do it for the amazing exhilaration of singing, the feeling of the music going through you."

Jan Howard

Singer, songwriter and author Jan Howard has seen her share of ups and downs personally and professionally and has managed to come out on top.

Born in West Plains, Missouri, Jan was married by age 16 and a mother of three boys by age 21. Her musical training was limited to singing along to country music on the radio. Divorced at age 24, the single mother worked as a waitress to support her young sons. After remarrying, the family moved to Los Angeles in 1953. That marriage ended also, and Jan worked as a secretary. Through singer Wynn Stewart she met and later married up-and-coming songwriter Harlan Howard.

She made demo records of Harlan's songs which got the attention of Johnny Bond and Tex Ritter who encouraged her when she first began recording. In 1959 she and Stewart recorded the duet "Yankee Go Home." That year, while in Nashville with her husband who was receiving a BMI award, she made her Opry debut at the Ryman Auditorium. The $65-a-week secretary had never sung on stage or before an audience when Ray Price first introduced her on the Opry.

The Howards moved from California to Nashville in 1960. Jan's first solo single "The One You Slip Around With" was a Top 10 hit and *Juke Box Operators*, *Billboard* and *Cash Box* magazines named her Most Promising Country/Western Vocalist.

In 1964 she signed with Decca Records. Produced by Owen Bradley, she had another hit in 1965 with "What Makes a Man Wander." That year she joined Bill Anderson's syndicated TV and road show and sang with him regularly on the Opry. For seven years they won many Duo of the Year awards. Their 1966 hit "For Loving You" was No. 1 for four weeks. "If It's All the Same to You," "We'll Be Together" and "Dis-Satisfied" were Top 5 hits.

At the same time, Jan's solo single "Evil on Your Mind" went Top 5, followed by "Bad Seed" which went Top 10. Her other chart successes included "Roll Over and Play Dead," "Count Your Blessings, Woman," "I Still Believe in Love," "When We Tried," "Rock Me Back to Little Rock" and "Spinning Wheel."

Jan's single "My Son" was released shortly after her eldest son Jimmy died in Vietnam in 1968. She writes about his death and that of her youngest son David four years later and how she coped with these personal tragedies in her 1987 autobiography *Sunshine and Shadow*.

In 1992, her efforts on behalf of the Armed Forces, mental health, the Veterans Administration, Vietnam Veterans and Vietnam Veterans Memorial earned Jan in 1992 the Tennessee Adjutant General's *Distinguished Patriot Medal*, its highest civilian honor.

A regular "guest" on the Opry for years, Jan "officially" joined the cast March 27, 1971. She still tours today and also works for causes related to military veterans. These days, Jan spends time off stage on the golf course.

THE $65-A-WEEK SECRETARY HAD NEVER SUNG ON STAGE OR BEFORE AN AUDIENCE WHEN RAY PRICE FIRST INTRODUCED JAN ON THE OPRY.

Jan finds two of her best Opry buddies backstage —Sonny Osborne and Jeannie Seely.

Alan Jackson

In 1985-86 when Alan Jackson was sorting the Opry stars' mail and carrying it from the TNN mail room to the Opry House, he only dreamed of having a hit record, selling albums, winning awards and singing on the Opry.

Those dreams of a country music career hadn't surfaced when he was growing up in Newnan, Georgia, the youngest of five children. The young Alan's only introduction to music was listening to his four sisters sing in church or school or watching *Hee Haw* every Saturday.

After graduating from high school, Alan worked at a variety of jobs, including driving a forklift, selling furniture, maintaining boats at a marina, selling shoes, working as a building contractor and repairing and selling cars. In his spare time, he began sitting in with local bands and writing songs. Soon the music bug bit, and he moved to Nashville. A chance meeting in the Atlanta airport between his wife Denise, then a flight attendant, and entertainer Glen Campbell led to Alan's signing on as a songwriter with Glen's music publishing company after the Jacksons moved to Music City in 1985.

From the outset, Alan wanted to write and sing real country music. Although he was turned down by every major label in town (and twice by some), in 1989 Arista Records signed Alan as the label's first country artist. He was off and running, recording 26 No. 1 hits in the 11 years since.

The influence of his favorite singers—George Jones, Merle Haggard and Hank Williams —is evident in his music. His string of hits, most of which he wrote or co-wrote, include "Here in the Real World," "Wanted," "Chasin' That Neon Rainbow," "Don't Rock the Jukebox," "Someday," "Chattahoochee," "Summertime Blues," "Livin' on Love,"

"Gone Country," "Right on the Money," "Tall, Tall Trees," "Little Bitty," "Who's Cheatin' Who" and "There Goes."

In 1999, Alan released *Under the Influence*, a collection of country and honky-tonk standards that influenced him, including a remake of fellow Opry star Jim Ed Brown's 1967 classic "Pop a Top."

Alan is keeping real country music alive— live on the Opry stage.

To date, Alan has sold more than 27 million albums. Since 1990, he's also collected more than 60 awards for his singing, songwriting and videos.

Alan joined the Opry on June 7, 1991.

When he isn't touring with his band the Strayhorns, he can be found fishing, boating and tinkering with cars, motorcycles, boats and anything with a motor. He collects classic cars, boats and Harley-Davidson motorcycles.

Alan Jackson has come a long way in the past few years, but he's just as humble as he was when he delivered mail to the Opry House. Today, he remains true to his commitment to keep real country music alive and help fill the shoes of his Opry heroes.

Stonewall Jackson

Yes, Stonewall is his real name. And the story of his rise to fame is as real a country music story as you find in the country archives anywhere. His true story measures up to the most unusual fictional account anyone could imagine.

Stonewall and Bill prepare to go live on TNN.

Born in Tabor City, North Carolina, the youngest of three children, he lost his father when he was only two. His mother decided to move to south Georgia to her brother-in-law's farm to find work.

Times were hard, so hard the family had to hitchhike to Georgia. After years working on the farm, Stonewall changed his birth records so he could join the Army at age 16. But, the Army found out and released him. At 17 he joined the Navy where he learned to play guitar and sing. When his stint was up in 1954, he decided on a new career—singing. But first he headed back to the farm to work and save for a new pickup. When he got it, Stonewall headed for Nashville.

First stop was an audition with Wesley Rose of Acuff-Rose publishing company. Rose liked his songs and the singer. He called his friend George D. Hay and sent Stonewall down to WSM radio. Judge Hay listened to a couple of songs and signed him to a contract.

On November 3, 1956, Stonewall joined the Opry.

WHEN HIS STINT WAS UP IN 1954, HE DECIDED ON A NEW CAREER—SINGING. BUT FIRST HE HEADED BACK TO THE FARM TO WORK AND SAVE FOR A NEW PICKUP. WHEN HE GOT IT, STONEWALL HEADED FOR NASHVILLE.

As Stonewall tells it, "Ernest Tubb, Roy Acuff and the management of the Opry lent me a hand when I needed one the most. I had no record. I was poor. I had no amount of money, no record contract and I didn't even have a decent guitar. I borrowed one for quite some time from other acts on the show."

Rose and Judge Hay knew exactly what they were doing. Maybe he wasn't a star when he was signed but he didn't waste any time. Soon he had a contract with Columbia, a relationship that lasted 18 years, and the hits began.

"Life to Go" became his first No. 1 hit in 1959. The next year "Waterloo" topped the pop and country charts. Twelve more No. 1 songs followed including "A Wound Time Can't Erase," "Leona," "BJ the DJ," "Angry Words," "Don't Be Angry," "Greener Pastures" and "Me and You and a Dog Named Boo." He has had 10 gold singles, five gold albums, 52 chart singles, 22 Top 10 hits, and 14 No. 1 songs.

This 40-year Opry star was honored in 1996 by the Country Gospel Music Association for the song "Jesus Is My Lifeline," which spent a record-breaking four months at No. 1 on the *Music City News Gospel Voice* charts. Stonewall wrote the song and sang it as a duet with country gospel artist Don Richmond.

On July 25, 1997, he was presented the Ernest Tubb Memorial Award for his outstanding contributions to the country music industry.

In 1991, Stonewall completed his autobiography entitled *From the Bottom Up*. He still performs with his band, the Minutemen, all across America, traveling the highways in his Silver Eagle Bus.

Jim & Jesse

IN A 1997

WHITE HOUSE CEREMONY,

JIM & JESSE RECEIVED

THE NATIONAL HERITAGE

FELLOWSHIP, THE

NATIONAL ENDOWMENT

FOR THE ARTS' MOST

PRESTIGIOUS HONOR

IN FOLK AND

TRADITIONAL ARTS.

In bluegrass music, Jim and Jesse McReynolds are two of the genre's most revered musicians. With a professional career spanning more than 50 years, they are certainly at the top of any bluegrass fan's list.

Jim and Jesse were born into a musical family. Their parents were talented musicians and their grandfather, a fiddler, made a recording for Victor Records about the time Jim was born.

Both learned to play stringed instruments and as teen agers honed their unmistakable harmony by singing traditional mountain music at folk gatherings—Jim the polished tenor and guitarist and younger brother (by two years) Jesse whose distinctive style of mandolin playing has to become known as "McReynolds" or "cross-picking."

The boys made their radio debut on a Virginia station in 1947 and moved to a Lexington, Kentucky, station in 1952. The same year they signed their first recording contract with Capitol Records.

Jim and Jesse's reputation grew as they performed at major bluegrass and folk festivals and on radio and television throughout the south.

Songs like "Are You Missing Me," "Border Ride," "Sweet Little Miss Blue Eyes," "I Wish You Knew," "Drifting and Dreaming of You," "Ole Slew Foot," "Freight Train," "Ballad of Thunder Road," "Cotton Mill Man," "Better Times A' Coming," "Diesel on my Tail" and "Paradise" established them as one of the world's leading duos.

They became Opry members on March 2, 1964.

Jim and Jesse also recorded more than 30 albums on Epic Records, Opryland Records and their own label Old Dominion. They received a 1998 Grammy nomination for their *Songs From the Homeplace*. In 1999, Pinecastle Records released a four CD boxed set titled *The Ole Dominion Masters*.

They were honored with a star in the Country Music Hall of Fame's Walkway of Stars and membership in Bill Monroe's Bluegrass Hall of Fame, the Virginia Country Music Hall of Fame and the International Bluegrass Music Association's Hall of Honor. In a 1997 White House ceremony, they received the *National Heritage Fellowship*, the National Endowment for the Arts' most prestigious honor in folk and traditional arts.

Jim and Jesse have taken their bluegrass harmony and music around the world appearing several times at the Wembley Festival in London as well as performing in Switzerland, France, Holland, Ireland, Austria, Sweden and Germany. They even recorded an album titled *Jim and Jesse— Live in Japan.*

Jesse says, "I don't think any musical brother or family group has ever stayed together actively for 50 years. So, it's possible that we may have set a record in that category." As Jim adds, "We'd like to think we've contributed something to the music world that might be beneficial to others and worthy of remembrance in the history of country and bluegrass music."

Jim and Jesse, accompanied by their Virginia Boys band, still tour and appear frequently at the many bluegrass festivals throughout the year in addition to their regular Opry appearances.

It's all in the family. Jim & Jesse play a bluegrass standard with the help of Jesse's grandson, Luke McKnight.

George Jones

When country music singers list their influences, George Jones is usually near the top. Few entertainers achieve the legendary status that George has reached. Though many often try to imitate him, no one has yet to duplicate him.

George, born in southeast Texas near Beaumont, grew up the eighth child in a poor family. He was introduced to music early by his mother, a church pianist, and his truck-driver/pipefitter father who played guitar. He came to music early, singing at 9, playing guitar at age 11, and writing his first song at 12. Soon he was picking, singing, writing and performing with a group of his own. By the age of 16, he had a regular spot on a Jasper, Texas, radio station.

He joined the Marines, but after three years he returned to Texas to pursue his musical career. He began his recording career with Starday Records in 1954 and had his first big hit "Why, Baby, Why" in 1955. Two years later he moved to Mercury, where he recorded "White Lightnin'," his first No. 1 record. Other hits during this era include "Window Up Above," "She Thinks I Still Care," "The Race Is On," "Walk Through This World With Me" and "The Grand Tour."

George joined the Opry on January 4, 1969.

Later that year, George married country superstar Tammy Wynette. Though the marriage ended in divorce four years later, they enjoyed chart success with "We're Gonna Hold On," "Golden Ring," "Near You" and "Two Story House."

One of the Opry's Hall of Famers, George Jones sings an award-winning hit.

George topped the charts twice in the 1980s with "He Stopped Loving Her Today" (1980) —which was named the Country Music Association's (CMA) Single of the Year in 1980 and 1981—and "Yesterday's Wine" (with Merle Haggard in 1982).

In 1992, George was inducted into the Country Music Hall of Fame. The Academy of Country Music awarded him its Pioneer Award.

In 1993, George enlisted the help of some of his friends and admirers—including Garth Brooks, Clint Black, Alan Jackson, Patty Loveless, Travis Tritt and others—for "I Don't Need Your Rockin' Chair," which claimed the CMA's Vocal Event of the Year Award.

George put his life and career into words with his 1996 autobiography *I Lived To Tell It All.*

In 1999, he released *Cold Hard Truth* that included the hit single "Choices," which won a Grammy for Best Male Country Vocal Performance.

So who were the country music singers that provided the inspiration for George Jones? "My favorites were Roy Acuff, and then Hank Williams and Lefty Frizzell," he says. "I got a lot of my phrasing from Lefty. You know, you make a five-syllable word out of a one-syllable. Then you add a little bit of Roy Acuff and a little bit from Hank Williams. I sing with my voice and their phrasing, and I thank those three people every day."

George tours throughout the country and resides just south of Nashville with his wife Nancy.

Hal Ketchum

Hal Ketchum considers himself a poet. He just sets his poems to music in the form of songs.

When Hal joined the Grand Ole Opry family on January 22, 1994, he wrote a poem for the occasion which read in part:

A thousand souls and singers have beckoned me to this hallowed place. And tho' some would say I've come a long way, I would say simply that tonight, I arrive.

The Greenwich, New York, native arrived at the Opry on the strength of several of those poem/songs, including his No. 2 hit "Small Town Saturday Night," the song that launched his career in mid-1991. Other hits included "I Know Where Love Lives," "Past The Point of Rescue," "Five O'Clock World," "Sure Love," "Hearts Are Gonna Roll," "Mama Knows the Highway," "(Tonight We Just Might) Fall in Love Again" and "Stay Forever."

Hal entertains the Opry audience by reading a poem he wrote to be recited on the night of his Opry induction.

Hal grew up in upstate New York listening to the music of Marty Robbins, Ray Charles, Buck Owens, Patsy Cline, Ernie Ford and Roger Miller. He started playing drums at age 15 but later switched to guitar. Although he enjoyed music, Hal was a carpenter and furniture builder for nearly 20 years before getting his break in the music business.

His success as a songwriter-singer came after he moved to Nashville by way of Texas. Hal left New York for Austin, Texas, in 1981, and it was there he played in local clubs and

honed his songwriting skills. He recorded an album of 10 original songs called *Threadbare Alibis* in 1986. At the same time he made periodic trips to Nashville to break into the singing and songwriting business there.

Intent on making a living as a songwriter, he initially signed a publishing contract with Curb Records. His first single "Small Town Saturday Night" from his debut album *Past the Point of Rescue* was named the No. 1 Single of the Year by *Radio and Records* magazine and the breakthrough video of the year by *Music Row* magazine. The song also helped the album achieve gold status.

Hal's subsequent albums produced hit after hit. He wrote a dozen new songs for an album titled *Hal, Yes* but the album release was put on hold in 1997. Five of those songs came out on his *I Saw the Light* CD in 1998. *Hal, Yes* was retitled *Awaiting Redemption* and was released in 1999.

After writing those songs and recording them, Hal was diagnosed with a neurological disorder called acute transverse myelitis in April 1998. He is recovering from the debilitating illness and recently moved from Texas to Chicago where he hosted a radio show called *Troubadours*. The one-hour musical talk show, produced by his wife Gina, aired on National Public Radio.

Hal also is studying acting in addition to writing and recording his beloved songs—poetry set to music.

Alison Krauss

When Alison Krauss joined the Opry family on July 3, 1993, not only did the Opry cast get a talented fiddler and singer, it also got bass, guitar, mandolin, dobro and banjo players. That's because Alison's band Union Station is part of the package.

The band includes Barry Bales, acoustic bass; Ron Block, banjo and acoustic guitar; Dan Tyminski, acoustic guitar and mandolin; and Jerry Douglas, dobro. All blend their voices with Alison, a championship fiddler. When Alison joined the Opry, she was the first bluegrass artist in 29 years to be inducted. Just shy of her 22nd birthday, she also was the youngest current cast member.

Alison was just 17 and already a veteran performer when she and Union Station made their first Opry appearance in 1989. They have since performed on the show numerous times and always enthrall Opry audiences with tight harmonies, superb musicianship and Alison's delicate and captivating voice.

The Champaign, Illinois, native started classical violin lessons at age 5. Turning to bluegrass at age 8, she soon was competing in and winning fiddling competitions. At 14, she recorded her first album *Too Late to Cry*. By age 18, she earned a Grammy nomination for her 1989 release *Two Highways* featuring Union Station. The following year, Alison won the Grammy for Best Bluegrass Recording for *I've Got That Old Feeling*.

Alison Krauss and Union Station won a second Grammy in 1992 for *Every Time You Say Goodbye*. Since 1992, Alison has garnered eight more Grammy Awards. In addition, she has been honored for her collaborations with the Cox Family "I Know Who Holds Tomorrow," Shenandoah ("Somewhere in the Vicinity of the Heart") and Vince Gill ("High Lonesome Sound").

I've Got That Old Feeling was named the International Bluegrass Music Association's (IBMA) 1991 Album of the Year. In 1992 the IBMA awarded her Album of the Year honors for *Every Time You Say Goodbye*. Alison is a four-time IBMA Female Vocalist of the Year winner and has twice received Entertainer of the Year honors.

The accolades continued for Alison at the 1995 Country Music Association Awards when she took home four trophies—Vocal Event with Shenandoah for "Somewhere in the Vicinity of the Heart," Single of the Year for "When You Say Nothing at All," Female Vocalist and the Horizon Award.

When they aren't working together, Alison Krauss and Union Station members pursue other projects, whether playing and producing sessions with other artists or writing songs. Alison has produced bluegrass albums for the Cox Family and Nickel Creek. Always in demand for studio work, Alison has sung and played on recordings by artists such as Alan Jackson, Kenny Rogers, Michael McDonald, Phish, Bad Company and Ralph Stanley.

In 1995, Alison's album *Now That I've Found You: A Collection* was certified double platinum. Alison Krauss & Union Station's 1997 *So Long So Wrong* has achieved gold status. *Forget About It*, her 1999 release, features guest vocalists Dolly Parton, Lyle Lovett and members of the Cox Family.

WHEN ALISON JOINED THE OPRY, SHE WAS THE FIRST BLUEGRASS ARTIST IN 29 YEARS TO BE INDUCTED. JUST SHY OF HER 22ND BIRTHDAY, SHE ALSO WAS THE YOUNGEST CURRENT CAST MEMBER.

Alison Krauss' Opry appearances feature her talented band Union Station—(left to right) Jerry Douglas Barry Bales, Dan Tyminski and Ron Block.

Hank Locklin

Nobody loves a great tenor like the Irish. No wonder Hank Locklin has been the number one country singer in Ireland for many years. He is certainly proclaimed as one of the great tenors of country music.

"I've never kissed the Blarney Stone," he admits. But that hasn't hurt his "luck of the Irish" when it comes to hits and awards.

Born Lawrence Hankins Locklin into a family that usually reared doctors, Hank was picking guitar for amateur contests in Milton, Florida, by age 10. In his teens he was a featured performer on Pensacola radio station WCOA.

Hank harmonizes with Carol Lee Cooper.

For the next several years he played with a variety of groups through the south and worked at various jobs in Florida—including farmer, ribbon mill hanker and shipyard worker.

After World War II ended, his career started taking off, and he appeared on Shreveport's Louisiana Hayride and the Dallas Big D Jamboree. He recorded briefly for Decca, and after meeting producer Bill McCall, Hank recorded for McCall's Four Star Records for five years.

Hank scored his first Top 10 song in 1949 with "The Same Sweet Girl." Four years later he had a No. 1 with "Let Me Be the One" and a recording contract with RCA Victor followed.

The next year he had a Top 5 with "Send Me the Pillow You Dream On," which he wrote, and a Top 3 hit with "It's a Little More Like Heaven/Blue Grass Skirt."

In 1960 he went to the top of the charts with "Please Help Me I'm Falling" which stayed at No. 1 on the country charts for 26 weeks and crossed over to the Top 10 pop charts both in the United States and the United Kingdom.

Other hits followed in the '60s—"One Step Ahead of My Time," "From Here to There to You," "Happy Birthday to Me," "You're the Reason," "Happy Journey," "We're Gonna Go Fishin,'" "Followed Closely By My Teardrops" and "The Country Hall of Fame."

Hank joined the Grand Ole Opry roster on November 9, 1960.

In addition to a list of awards for "Send Me the Pillow That You Dream On," he has an ASCAP Award for the album *Country Hall of Fame*. He also has *Cashbox* and *Juke Box* magazine awards for "Please Help Me I'm Falling" and a NARAS Award for *Locklin Sings Hank Williams*.

Hank helped pioneer the idea of a concept album—*Foreign Love, Irish Songs, Country Style* are examples.

He has recorded more than 38 albums, and his songs recently were released in the new *Please Help Me I'm Falling* collection.

Charlie Louvin

Charlie Louvin is no stranger to hit songs, whether he's singing them or writing them for others to perform. In fact, he and his brother Ira, who died in a tragic car crash in 1965, wrote more than 500 songs, a feat that led to their induction into the Songwriters Hall of Fame in 1979.

The Louvin Brothers didn't start out as songwriters and singers. Born Charlie and Ira Loudermilk in Alabama's Sand Mountain region, early on they worked in the cotton fields and later the cotton mills. When they weren't doing farm chores, they learned to play guitar and started singing together. The teen-age brothers' unique harmony earned them first prize in an amateur talent contest—a chance to perform on a radio show broadcast daily at 4 a.m. on Chattanooga's WDEF.

The brothers kept their day jobs and performed on the side during the mid-1940s. Their career stalled somewhat while Charlie was in the Army, but once he got out, they worked for radio stations in Knoxville and Memphis. Brief stints recording for Decca and MGM yielded little success. With help from Fred Rose, whose Acuff-Rose company published their songs, the Louvin Brothers signed with Capitol Records and released "The Family Who Prays" which became a gospel standard.

The Army recalled Charlie during the Korean conflict, but after his military service ended, the two brothers relaunched their performing career at a Birmingham radio station. Thanks to some help from Capitol Records, the Grand Ole Opry gave the Louvin Brothers a chance in February 1955, and this time their career took off both in sacred and secular music circles.

That year "When I Stop Dreaming" was a Top 10 hit and stayed on the charts for 13 weeks. The next year they scored a No. 1 hit with "I Don't Believe You've Met My Baby," followed by the Top 10 hits "Hoping That You're Hoping" and "You're Running Wild."

Charlie and Ira decided to pursue solo careers in 1963. One of Charlie's first releases, "I Don't Love You Anymore," was a Top 10 hit in 1964. Other Top 10 successes included "Will You Visit Me on Sunday," "Mama's Angels," "Funny Man," "When You Fly Alone" and "See The Big Man Cry."

In 1970 and 1971 Charlie and Melba Montgomery were successful with duets such as "Something to Brag About" and "Baby, You've Got What It Takes." In 1979, he also recorded "Love Don't Care" with Emmylou Harris (whose first No. 1 hit was a remake of the Louvin Brothers "If I Could Only Win Your Love"). In 1989 Charlie teamed up with Roy Acuff to record and produce a video of Roy's 1940 classic "The Precious Jewel." That same year he recorded the album *Charlie Louvin 50 Years of Makin' Music* which featured him singing with Montgomery, Willie Nelson, Waylon Jennings, George Jones, Charlie Daniels, Crystal Gayle and Tanya Tucker.

Today, Charlie, a 45-year Opry member, continues to promote the music he and his brother created. For many years he hosted the "May on the Mountain Bluegrass Festival" at the Louvin Brothers Music Park in Henagar, Alabama. In 1996 he moved the Louvin Brothers Museum to Bell Buckle, Tennessee. He received the 1997 Heritage Award at the annual Uncle Dave Macon Days in Murfreesboro, Tennessee.

THE LOUVIN BROTHERS

DIDN'T START OUT

AS SONGWRITERS

AND SINGERS...

THEY WORKED IN THE

COTTON FIELDS AND

LATER THE COTTON MILLS.

Charlie Louvin sings one of the 500 songs he wrote with his late brother Ira.

Patty Loveless

Patty visits the Opry stage during its holiday season.

GROWING UP IN A

HOUSEHOLD OF MUSIC

LOVERS, PATTY WAS

INFLUENCED BY

ALL KINDS OF MUSIC.

Patty Loveless remembers listening to the Opry when she was just three years old. On Friday and Saturday nights, she would sing along while her mother mopped the floors. For Patty, the Opry was her connection to the world that she dreamed about exploring someday.

Country music fans are glad Patty followed her dream.

Patty grew up the youngest girl in a house with seven children. She was singing by age 5 and at age 12, she was singing the songs of Connie Smith, Dolly Parton, Merle Haggard, George Jones and Elvis.

Growing up in a household of music lovers, she was influenced by all kinds of music—the pure Appalachian sounds of her native Kentucky to the rock 'n' roll and big band she heard coming out of the records her brothers and sisters were playing.

"My father loved the mountain bluegrass sound of the Stanley Brothers, Lester Flatt & Earl Scruggs and Bill Monroe. He took me to see Lester, Earl & the Foggy Mountain Boys perform on top of a concession stand during an intermission at a local drive-in theater. I was only six years old and I can still remember that moment to this day," Patty recalls.

She traveled to Nashville at the age of 14 where she auditioned for Porter Wagoner. Soon after, she was hired by the Wilburn Brothers to replace their departing "girl singer" Loretta Lynn (a distant cousin of Patty's) and as a staff songwriter. During this time, the "girl singer" was realizing her dreams.

Marriage and a move to North Carolina interrupted the climb to stardom but she returned to Nashville in the mid-'80s and released her first album *Patty Loveless* in 1986.

If My Heart Had Windows followed and the title song became her first Top 10. She joined the Opry on June 11, 1988 just after the album's release.

Patty married producer Emory Gordy Jr. in 1989 and together they have crafted a body of work that is unparalleled in Nashville.

Patty's first No. 1 song, "Timber (I'm Falling in Love)," came from her *Honky Tonk Angel* album which also produced the chart-topping single "Chains." "Blue Side of Town," "Don't Toss Us Away" and "Lonely Side of Love" each made it to the Top 10.

"Blame It On Your Heart," "How Can I Help You Say Goodbye?" "Here I Am," "You Don't Even Know Who I Am," "Halfway Down," "You Can Feel Bad" and "Lonely Too Long" are some of her nine No. 1 songs.

She was the Academy of Country Music's Top Female Vocalist in 1996 and 1997. She won the Country Music Association's Female Vocalist of the Year honors in 1996, and the Album of the Year trophy in 1995 for *When Fallen Angels Fly*. Three times she has captured the Vocal Event of the Year category, twice with George Jones (1993, 1995) and once with Vince Gill (1999).

Patty recently released her second greatest hits collection simply titled *Patty Loveless Classics*.

Loretta Lynn

The name Loretta Lynn is almost as big as country music itself.

Fans around the world know well the story of her poor childhood in the coal mining area of Van Lear, Kentucky. They know that she was named for movie star Loretta Young, didn't walk until she was four, and almost died three times.

Her best-selling autobiography *Coal Miner's Daughter* and the 1980 movie that won an Oscar for actress Sissy Spacek shared the entertainer's story and made Loretta Lynn a household name.

"Sing it, sister." Loretta takes center stage, flanked by sisters Peggy Sue Wright and Crystal Gayle.

Loretta quit school after the eighth grade and married O.V. "Mooney" Lynn when she was only 13 years old. It was love at first sight when Loretta saw her "Doolittle," or "Doo" as she often called him. He bought her homemade pie at a school social and weeks later, they were married.

A move to Washington and motherhood followed. As Loretta sang to her babies, Doo listened and knew that his wife had a gift. He landed her a job with a local band on Saturday nights and entered her in a talent contest hosted by Buck Owens.

The owner of Zero Records saw her and helped her record one of her self-penned songs, "Honky Tonk Girl." Thanks to the efforts of Loretta and Mooney—who drove from radio station to radio station getting DJs to play "Girl"—the song went to No. 14. Loretta and her family moved to Nashville.

LORETTA'S HITS HAVE MADE HER ONE OF THE MOST INFLUENTIAL FEMALE VOCALISTS AND SONGWRITERS OF ALL TIME.

The Wilburn Brothers took notice and got her a guest spot on the Grand Ole Opry in October 1960. She was introduced to the audience by Ernest Tubb for what she still remembers as "the best moment of my life." She signed with Decca Records, and her first Decca single "Success" hit the Top 10.

She joined the Opry cast September 25, 1962.

In the next decade she ruled the charts with 59 hits as a solo artist—22 of them in the Top 10—and 18 more with duet partners Ernest Tubb and Conway Twitty.

Along the way hits such as "You Ain't Woman Enough," "The Pill," "Don't Come Home A Drinkin'," "One's On The Way," "Love Is The Foundation," "Blue Kentucky Girl" and "Out of My Head and Back In My Bed" helped make her one of the most influential female vocalists and songwriters of all time. And Opry audiences still rise to their feet after Loretta's delivery of her signature song "Coal Miner's Daughter."

In addition to becoming the first female Country Music Association Entertainer of the Year she has won dozens of other major awards including Female Vocalist of the Year and the Academy of Country Music's 1975 Entertainer of the Year. She and Twitty were repeatedly named Duo of the Year and in 1985, in Los Angeles, she received the American Music Award of Merit in recognition of her exemplary career in music —a career that was bigger than country—for the power and inspiration of her distinctive music. Membership in the Country Music Hall of Fame followed in 1988.

Following Doo's death in 1996, she has continued to live in their Hurricane Mills, Tennessee, home and tourist attraction, which they purchased in 1966. She continues to record, tour, and visit the Opry, often joining her singing daughters the Lynns on the Opry stage.

Barbara Mandrell

Barbara Mandrell has spent a lifetime in the spotlight.

She was born in Houston on Christmas Day to Irby and Mary Mandrell—musical parents who taught her to read music before she could read words. She was playing complicated pieces such as "Gospel Boogie" on the accordion when she was still in ruffled socks. She took up the pedal steel and saxophone and made her showbiz debut at age 10 on Cousin Herb Henson's Bakersfield TV and radio show.

What was supposed to be only a job demonstrating musical instruments with her dad at a trade show turned into an audition for Chet Atkins and "Uncle" Joe Maphis, and she soon joined Maphis performing at the Vegas Showboat. She became a regular on the Los Angeles TV show *Town Hall Party* and went on to Red Foley's ABC-TV show *Five Star Jubilee* and joined a concert tour with Johnny Cash, Patsy Cline, George Jones and June Carter.

Soon afterward, she was touring the world with mom and dad as "The Mandrells." They hired a young drummer named Ken Dudney for their act, and when he received his Navy pilot wings, Barbara became his wife. He left for overseas, and Barbara left her career to be a housewife.

Barbara's family—Jamie Nicole, Barbara, Ken, Matthew and Nathan (front center)

But she was born for the spotlight. One night while visiting the Opry, she whispered in her dad's ear, "Daddy, I wasn't cut out to be in the audience."

She was right. Within 48 hours of her appearance in a club near the Opry she received six recording contract offers. She

signed with CBS and introduced her trademark blue-eyed soul style by releasing the old Ottis Redding classic "I've Been Loving You Too Long." She joined the Opry on July 29, 1972.

Her first No. 1 hit was "Burning the Midnight Oil" in 1973. She continued the hits with "Standing Room Only," "Sleeping Single in a Double Bed," "Married, But Not to Each Other," "Years" and "If Loving You Is Wrong (I Don't Want To Be Right)." In 1979 she was the Country Music Association's (CMA) Female Vocalist of the Year, and for the next two years she and her two sisters were the stars of the popular TV music variety show *Barbara Mandrell and the Mandrell Sisters*.

Her success soared. She was the first artist to win CMA Entertainer of the Year honors two years in a row.

On the evening of September 11, 1984, Barbara and two of her children narrowly escaped death when a young driver's car drifted across two lanes and hit them head on. Only minutes before she had buckled all their seat belts. There were two years of pain and physical therapy, but she made a full recovery and came back with a live performance at the Universal Amphitheater in Los Angeles on February 28, 1986.

A guest appearance on the TV show *The Commish* sparked her interest in acting and she began appearing in television series. She has since left behind the music arena for the most part to concentrate on appearances on *Touched by An Angel*, *Baywatch*, *Diagnosis Murder*, *Dr. Quinn Medicine Woman* and many other series and specials.

Barbara Mandrell—singer, musician, actress. Born to be in the spotlight.

Martina McBride

IN 1990 MARTINA WAS

WORKING AS A

WAITRESS, SINGING ON

DEMO TAPES AND

SELLING T-SHIRTS FOR

GARTH BROOKS' TOUR.

When Martina McBride walked to the stage to pick up her 1999 CMA Female Vocalist of the Year award, the humble performer seemed genuinely surprised. No one else was. Martina's was a voice whose time had come.

In 1990 she was working as a waitress, singing on demo tapes and selling T-shirts for Garth Brooks' tour.

By the end of the decade, she'd become known for incendiary delivery and impeccable sense of song, sold millions of records and headlined her own sold-out shows.

Born Martina Schiff in Sharon, Kansas, she learned country music when her father, a farmer with his own part-time band, taught her classics such as Patsy Cline's "I Fall to Pieces" and Jeanne Pruett's "Satin Sheets." Martina started singing with him when she was 7. "Dad played acoustic guitar and sang. I sang with him. Mom ran the soundboard. It was a family thing to do. It was quite an upbringing. Every Saturday night we played dances," she remembers. "I always felt like singing was what I was put here to do."

As soon as she was out of high school, Martina began singing seriously. She went to Hutchinson, Kansas, and sang with a band there for a year and a half. Soon she decided to form her own band and rented a rehearsal studio from a sound system operator named John McBride.

A relationship bloomed and they were married in 1988. The couple moved to

Husband John looks on as Martina does her own typing during an Opry.com backstage chat.

Nashville in early 1990, and in 1991, John went on tour with Garth Brooks as his production manager. Martina went along and sold T-shirts for the tour.

Two years later, after signing with RCA, she became Garth's opening act performing songs from her first album, *The Time Has Come.*

The following year her second album, *The Way That I Am*, went platinum and yielded two Top 10 hits, "My Baby Loves Me" and "Life No 9" plus "Independence Day," which won video awards from nearly every country trade association in the book.

Martina became a member of the Grand Ole Opry on November 30, 1995, during the taping of its 70th Anniversary CBS special. "I never thought it would happen," she said. "It's so incredible. Whenever I do the Opry it still feels like the first time. I still get nervous. The Opry's going to be here for hundreds of years and I'm just proud my name is on that list. It's a highlight of my life. An amazing honor."

Martina's star has been on a continuous rise since her Opry induction. Her subsequent albums—*Wild Angels, Evolution* and *Emotion*—have all sold more than a million copies and have included hits such as "Safe In The Arms Of Love," "A Broken Wing," "Whatever You Say," "I Love You," "Love's The Only House" and "There You Are."

Martina has showcased her songs on network television shows from *Good Morning America* to *The Tonight Show With Jay Leno*, and she's made cameo appearances on series such as *General Hospital, Early Edition* and *Baywatch*, where she was cast as an aspiring country singer—a role she knew well before hitting the big time, including that Female Vocalist of the Year honor, which surprised no one but her.

Mel McDaniel

Mel McDaniel became a member of the Opry on January 11, 1986, just three days before the *Opry's 60th Anniversary Special* on CBS-TV. That special closed with a hit Mel had written for Country Music Hall of Famer Conway Twitty in 1978— "Grandest Lady of Them All." The song that pays tribute to the Grand Ole Opry was written long before Mel had a personal connection to the Opry and certainly before the singer/songwriter/guitarist ever fathomed he'd become a member of the Opry's elite cast.

Mel grew up in Oklahoma and decided to pursue a career in music after seeing Elvis on TV. At age 14 he taught himself the guitar chords to "Frankie and Johnny" and first performed publicly at age 15 when he entered a high school talent contest.

After graduation he married and resided briefly in Nashville before taking a cue from a Johnny Horton hit, heading north to Alaska. He honed his talents and began playing to packed houses in Anchorage. Two years later he was back in Nashville and landed a job as a demo singer and songwriter with Combine Music through the efforts of renowned music publisher Bob Beckham.

In 1976 he signed with Capitol Records, and his debut single "Have A Dream On Me" was an instant success.

"Dream" was followed by a string of Top 10 hits, including "Louisiana Saturday Night," "Right In The Palm Of Your Hand," "I Call It Love," "Stand Up," "Real Good Feel Good Song," "Take Me to the Country," "Stand on It," "Big Ole Brew," "Ole Man River (I've Come to Talk to You Again)," "Let It Roll" and others.

While his distinctive voice was being heard on country radio across the nation, his songwriting talent was producing hits for others, as well. Hoyt Axton was the first to record one of his songs, "Roll Your Own." Mel and Dennis Linde wrote "Goodbye Marie," which was included on a million-selling Kenny Rogers album.

And even with hit after hit of his own and top tunes penned for others, Mel will be the first to tell Opry fans that wherever he travels, it is his 1984 chart-topper "Baby's Got Her Blue Jeans On" that fans remember most of all. The tune earned Grammy and CMA award nominations and essentially did what Mel always said he wanted to do. "I wanted to be a singer because I wanted to make people feel good with my music."

Taking a line from his hit song, Mel McDaniel "stands up" for the Opry crowd.

Reba McEntire

From her spectacular stage shows, national commercials and movies to her No. 1 hits, this redheaded rodeo girl from Oklahoma has rocked the world of country music for more than two decades.

The daughter of a school teacher and an Oklahoma rancher, Reba, the third of four children, grew up in a family of achievers. Her father and grandfather were world-champion steer ropers and she traveled the rodeo quarter-horse, barrel-racing circuit.

At the National Finals Rodeo in Oklahoma City in 1975, Reba sang the national anthem. Red Steagall heard her and advised her to visit Nashville and make a demo. Her first traditional country album failed to hit the Top 40 and she returned home to complete her teaching degree.

But with determination, Reba made it back to Nashville and landed a recording deal that would eventually propel her to superstar status.

Among her memorable songs are "I Can't Even Get The Blues," "You're The First Time I've Thought About Leaving," "Whoever's In New England," "For My Broken Heart," "Fancy," "The Night The Lights Went Out In Georgia" and "Fallin' Out Of Love."

She has recorded more than 25 albums and sold more than 40 million of them to an ever-expanding world-wide audience.

Reba was the Country Music Association's Female Vocalist of the Year from 1984 to 1987 and Entertainer of the Year in 1986. She picked up Vocal Event of the Year honors with Linda Davis for "Does He Love You," and took home the American Music Award for Favorite Female Country Artist 1988 - 1996 and again in 1998. Indeed, she's won every major country award out there.

"I tend to center my songs for women," she says. "I know a song is right when I hear it, just like I know a dress is right when I put it on. The wonderful thing is that even though I look for songs that speak to women, I find that when women like them, the men like them too," she says.

Always at the forefront with new ideas for her show, her look, her songs, and her career, Reba admits that she likes change. "I change my show twice a year," she says. "If I don't have songs and a show that are creative and keep me interested, I'm in trouble. My momma said that when I was born, my attention span was zilch, and its gone downhill from there."

In the '90s her creative attention turned toward the big screen, and she's since appeared in feature films and several made-for TV movies.

A non-stop "do-er," Reba these days easily balances a more-than-full-time job with being a full-time mother. Her normal pace is full speed ahead. Any given month might find her touring, filming a movie or carpooling her son Shelby to Scouts or a hockey match.

When asked by a journalist recently why she didn't just sit back and enjoy all that she's worked so hard to achieve, the Opry member since January 14, 1986 said, "Now why would I want to do that? I have a job that I love. I meet interesting people every day of my life. And I get to sing. What more could a person want out of life?"

Four decades of CMA Female Vocalists of the Year get together backstage during the Opry's run at the Ryman Auditorium: Reba McEntire ('84 – '87), Loretta Lynn ('67, '72 – '73) and Patty Loveless ('96).

Ronnie Milsap

Folks say Ronnie Milsap's talent is as vast and multi-dimensional as the American South, having provided country music with one of its most important voices as the genre was moving beyond its rural roots into the mainstream of modern entertainment.

Steeped in the mountain music of his native North Carolina and schooled in classical piano, Ronnie found inspiration early in life from a wide variety of music. Even as he mastered Beethoven and Mozart, his heart belonged to hardcore country and rhythm-and-blues music he often heard on stations from Nashville, including WSM-AM.

40 No. 1s . . . and counting. Ronnie Milsap treats those in the Opry House to a classic, "Smoky Mountain Rain."

Born blind and into dire poverty, Ronnie lived with his grandmother from age 1 to 6. He was then sent to the Morehead State School for the Blind in Raleigh, where he faced harsh treatment throughout his grade school and high school years. All along, the sightless child took refuge in music and radio. While Morehead put him through strict classical music training, late at night he continued to listen to his favorite country, gospel and rhythm and blues programs.

Ronnie didn't guess that he'd one day become one of radio's all-time greatest success stories, racking up 40 No. 1 country hits. After completing high school in Raleigh, he attended Young-Harris Junior College near Atlanta and picked up jobs as a sideman in the area. Soon he

BORN BLIND AND INTO

DIRE POVERTY...RONNIE

DIDN'T GUESS THAT

HE'D ONE DAY BECOME

ONE OF RADIO'S

ALL-TIME GREATEST

SUCCESS STORIES.

formed a band and found steady work playing clubs and colleges.

In his early years he was a member of the J. J. Cale band and played on sessions. He played keyboards on Elvis' "Kentucky Rain" and sang harmony on "Don't Cry Daddy."

In 1969, he and his group moved to Memphis, Tennessee, and started working at T.J.'s, a popular Memphis club.

Then in 1973 Ronnie, his wife Joyce and son Todd moved to Nashville. Before you could say "overnight success" he was signed by RCA and released a two-sided hit, "All Together Now (Let's Fall Apart)" and "I Hate You."

He followed with "That Girl Who Waits On Tables" and "Pure Love" and was named CMA's Male Vocalist of the Year on three occasions.

Ronnie joined the Opry on February 6, 1976.

Amid the release of classics such as "Daydreams About Night Things," "(I'm A) Stand By My Woman Man," "Smoky Mountain Rain" and "Lost In The Fifties Tonight," Ronnie took home the CMA's most prestigious award, Entertainer of the Year.

He's enjoyed multiple gold and platinum albums and has the only gold braille album ever awarded.

While looking back on the enormous impact he had on country music in the '70s, '80s and early '90s, the ebullient singer insists on looking ahead, as well. "I've been very fortunate to have had a lot of successful records," he says. "Now this is the time to make some more."

Lorrie Morgan

"You can't imagine how it felt the night I became a member of the Opry on June 9, 1984," Lorrie Morgan says. "The first time I could really call this place my home. I couldn't stop shaking or trembling, or crying," Lorrie recalled.

It might have been her first night as a member, but it sure wasn't her first night at the Opry. Lorrie grew up backstage at the Opry—the daughter of Opry star and Country Music Hall of Fame inductee George Morgan, a member for 26 years and known everywhere for his smash 1949 hit "Candy Kisses."

Lorrie made her debut on the Opry stage early, introduced at the Ryman Auditorium by her proud father. "My little 13-year-old knees were absolutely knocking," she says. "But I saw Dad standing there just bawling, and those people gave me a standing ovation. I thought, "This is what I'm doing the rest of my life."

Always a crowd favorite, Lorrie made her Opry debut at age 13.

Her father died when she was 16, but not before sharing two pieces of advice Lorrie says she carries with her still today: "Never say 'I can't'" and "Always remember your manners."

In truth, there has been nothing Lorrie Morgan couldn't do throughout her successful career. Everything seemed to take off with the 1989 release of *Dear Me*. She won the CMA 1990 Vocal Event of the Year award for her work with late husband Keith Whitley, and her three subsequent albums—*Leave the Light On*, *Something in Red* and *Watch Me* went platinum.

She's released hit after hit in her own distinctive style of passion and believability —"I Guess You Had to Be There," "What Part of No," "Except for Monday," "Go Away," "I Didn't Know my Own Strength," "Half Enough" and others.

Throughout her career, Lorrie says she's always thought of the Opry as home. "The Opry gave me my start in country music," Lorrie says. "It's a place we all need to go from time to time to remember why we're here and what gave us the opportunity to be here."

Lorrie has recorded duets with everyone from Frank Sinatra and Johnny Mathis to Dolly Parton and Sammy Kershaw. When she is not on the road with her heavy tour schedule, the talented writer is spending time with her kids—daughter Morgan and son Jesse—in the studio taping demos for other artists, or at home on the Opry stage.

Jimmy C. Newman

BORN AND RAISED IN

TRUE CAJUN STYLE. . .

IT WASN'T CAJUN

MUSIC, BUT THE

COWBOY MUSIC OF

GENE AUTRY THAT HE

STARTED SINGING...

Jimmy C. Newman was born and raised in true Cajun style just outside of Big Mamou, Louisiana. However, it wasn't his Cajun music, but the cowboy music of his boyhood hero Gene Autry that he started singing with bands traveling through the South and Southwest. Soon he was hosting his own radio show in Lake Charles, Louisiana. That led to membership on the famous Shreveport radio and TV show, The Louisiana Hayride and a Dot Records recording contract.

In 1954 he got his first country hit— "Cry, Cry Darling," which he co-wrote. He followed that with the hits "Daydreamin" and "Blue Darlin" and was invited to join the Opry in August 1956.

In 1957 his hit "Fallen Star" went to No. 1 on the country charts then crossed over to pop.

Then it was time to get back to his Cajun roots. He formed his "Cajun Country" band and was soon playing the music of his native Louisiana to fans around the world. Along the way he became the only Cajun artist ever to receive a gold record on a Cajun French song. The tune, "Lache Pas La Potate," earned gold status in Canada in 1976.

"AAAA-EEEE!" Jimmy C. Newman helps another Cajun great Jo-El Sonnier celebrate a backstage birthday.

Jimmy and his band Cajun Country have enjoyed success in Europe since their first appearance in London, England, at the famous Wembley Country Music Festival in 1980.

In 1991, Jimmy C. and Cajun Country earned a Grammy nomination for their Rounder album *Alligator Man*. The next year, Jimmy C. earned a special award from the "Cajun French Music Association" of South Louisiana for contributions to the promotion of Cajun music worldwide.

No stranger to television, Jimmy C. has appeared on a number of music specials and, in November 1993, made a guest appearance in a CBS Sunday Night Movie called *Conviction*, playing and singing traditional Cajun Music.

On March 12, 2000, Jimmy was inducted into the North American Country Music Association's International Hall of Fame and proudly accepted the honor in Sevierville, Tennessee. That award hangs on the wall alongside his induction to the Cajun Music Hall of Fame in Lafayette, Louisiana. Jimmy C. is equally proud of his induction to Fred's Lounge "Wall of Fame" in his hometown.

Jimmy C. credits his band for much of his unique Cajun sound. With Bessyl Duhon on Cajun accordion and some of the very best musicians in Music City, the group often treats audiences to toe-tappers such as "Jole Blon," "Jambalaya" and "Diggy Diggy Lo." They still tour Europe at least once a year and play several concerts each year throughout the U.S. and Canada.

Jimmy C. and his wife, Mae, continue to make their home on their 670-acre "Singing Hills Ranch" in Rutherford Country, Tennessee, just a short drive from Music City and the Grand Ole Opry.

Osborne Brothers

Many a football fan is also a fan of the Osborne Brothers—they just might not know it. The brothers' bluegrass hit "Rocky Top," now an official state song of Tennessee, is also the pep song for the University of Tennessee sports.

But it's not just Tennessee Vols fans who stand up and take notice when the Osbornes share their unique musicianship and vocal style. When it comes to traditional, innovative, old-time songs and bluegrass, they rule as one of the most popular groups of the era.

Born in the coal mining region of Southeastern Kentucky, Bobby and Sonny were naturals singing "Nine Pound Hammer" and "The Knoxville Girl" as well as other mining songs and folk ballads of the Appalachian Mountains.

Because of a six-year age difference they didn't start out singing together as fans today have come to expect—Bobby with the distinctive and unequaled natural high lead voice playing mandolin and younger brother Sonny's rich baritone.

Sonny, an alumnus of the Bill Monroe "school of bluegrass," recorded with Mr. Bill's Blue Grass Boys on Decca and had several recordings of his own on the Gateway label before becoming a duo with his brother in 1953 following Bobby's discharge from the U.S. Marine Corps.

Sonny (left) and Bobby (right)—the Osborne Brothers treat the Opry audience to more of that high lonesome sound.

The brothers' recording debut came in 1956—recordings that continue to rank among the all-time classic examples of Osborne Brother style. It was on these recordings that they changed the customary arrangement of trio harmony parts to create a new and completely unique sound. The MGM releases of the late '50s clearly marked them as an important group in country music.

In 1963 they signed with Decca (now MCA) and became members of the Grand Ole Opry on August 8, 1964.

These Decca recordings established the successful practice of featuring the Osborne "big voice" sound while giving greatly increased prominence to the instrumental wizardry of the duo—Sonny and his five-string banjo and Bobby with his mandolin.

In addition to "Rocky Top," the brothers' hit records include "Making Plans," "Up This Hill and Down," "Midnight Flyer," "Take Me Home, Country Roads," "Muddy Bottom," "Tennessee Houndog," "Georgia Pineywoods" and "Ruby." And the Osbornes didn't limit themselves to just one state song. Their "Kentucky" has been named an official song of their home state.

The brothers from Hyden, Kentucky, headed back to the bluegrass state in 1994 for what is regarded as the highest honor in bluegrass, induction into the International Bluegrass Music Association's Hall of Honor. Perhaps if one had listened intently that night, he might have heard faint voices in the distance . . . "touchdown!"

Bashful Brother Oswald

BORN IN THE GREAT

SMOKY MOUNTAINS,

THE SON OF AN

APPALACHIAN MUSICIAN,

OS LEARNED GUITAR

AND BANJO

AS A YOUNGSTER.

When Bashful Brother Oswald stepped center stage wearing his bib overalls and trademark orange hat and became a member of the Opry on January 21, 1995, he had already been playing the Opry almost every weekend for more than 50 years.

Oswald—who had been one of the most respected dobro players in country music—had also been a member of Roy Acuff's Smoky Mountain Boys for half a century. Now he was an official member in his own right.

"I'm the happiest man alive. This is a wonderful honor for me," he said. Then, adding his howling trademark laugh, he joked, "You know, I've been auditioning for this part for 56 years!"

Born Beecher Ray Kirby, near Sevierville, Tennessee, in the Great Smoky Mountains, the son of an Appalachian musician, "Os" —as he's known to friends—learned guitar and banjo as a youngster. Later he played and passed the hat to supplement his sawmill income.

As a young man he took a job in a car factory in Flint, Michigan, and began playing guitar and banjo in small clubs. Hawaiian music was popular at the time and Os bought his first steel guitar to fit in with the craze that was flooding the radio station where he played live music. He performed at the Chicago World's Fair and the following year moved to Knoxville and began playing dobro with local bands. He met Roy Acuff in Knoxville and joined the Smoky Mountain Boys at the Opry on January 8, 1939.

In addition to playing dobro, guitar and banjo, he also sang tenor with Roy, played

Oswald treats 'em to his unique dobro stylings.

jug in the jug band and did comedy. When Rachel Veach joined the group, Kirby became her "great big Bashful Brother Oswald," and they performed together, singing, playing, and doing comedy routines.

Roy once said, "I don't think anyone has the style, the touch and the control of a dobro instrument like Oswald. I don't think anyone has ever come close to him in his type of playing. He also plays the banjo in the old clawhammer or mountain style. Os is the best."

Roy often showcased him as a featured artist and after Roy's death both Os and band member Charlie Collins performed regularly on the Opry.

Os played on most of Roy Acuff's recordings and sang on the classics "Precious Jewel" and "Wreck on the Highway." He also recorded his own albums including *Celebrating 25 Years with Roy Acuff* and *Bashful Brother Oswald*.

In 1990 he was awarded the Heritage Award at Uncle Dave Macon Days in Murfreesboro, Tennessee, and in 1994 he published his biography *That's The Truth If I've Ever Told It*.

The night he joined the Opry all of the Opry members on stage sang "Wabash Cannonball" and Oswald played along just as he had done for 56 years.

"I don't ever want to retire," he says. "I don't know what I'd retire on. Looks sure won't get it," he laughs.

And how would Roy Acuff have felt about Oswald joining the Opry? "I guess he would appreciate it a whole lot," says Oswald. "I'm sure he would."

Dolly Parton

Few stars are recognized in every corner of the land by their first name only. Dolly is one of them. Dolly's fans surround the globe and include some of country music's brightest stars.

Fellow Opry member Marty Stuart has said, "People and trends come and go. She remains steadfast and solid. She's timeless, beautiful and spiritual. The Bible says, 'Many are called, but few are chosen.' I think we all agree that she is a chosen one."

Mary Chapin Carpenter compares singing with the Opry legend to "singing with an angel," and upon completing her own recording project with the beloved entertainer, Alison Krauss said, "Nothing can top getting to sing with Dolly Parton. Now I can die."

Dolly, with her glamorous fashions, golden gossamer wigs, long nails, sparkling jewelry and lively wit, has always created a larger-than-life image wherever and whenever she has performed.

Her books, music, concerts, movie roles, Dollywood entertainment complex and cosmetic line have all contributed to making Dolly an internationally known and recognized mega-star.

Dolly Rebecca Parton was born the fourth of 12 children to a hard working farm couple Robert Lee and Avie Lee Parton in the impoverished East Tennessee hills of Sevier County at the foothills of the Great Smoky Mountain National Park.

True to her dreams, she headed for Nashville the day after high school graduation. On her first afternoon there, she met Carl Dean. Two years later, May 1966, they were married.

In 1967 the magic happened. Porter Wagoner put her on his syndicated television show, and its audience of 45 million people loved her style, her look and her music.

Dolly joined the Grand Ole Opry on January 4, 1969, began enjoying solo hits, and became a superstar. In 1974, she decided it was time for a major change in her career and left the *Porter Wagoner Show* to pursue a world of other opportunities.

Those opportunities landed her CMA's top honors, Grammy awards, movie roles, television shows, book deals and more.

She's written many of her own hits, including "I Will Always Love You," which she took to the top of the country charts twice and with which Whitney Houston enjoyed a world-wide smash. Opry buddy Vince Gill recorded a duet of the song with Dolly, and it landed the pair a CMA Award.

Her Dollywood Foundation has provided nearly two million dollars for education in her home county, and her hometown has honored her with a bronze sculpture on the lawn of the Sevierville Courthouse.

In 1999, Dolly joined the ranks of the Country Music Hall of Fame. Upon hearing of her latest achievement, Dolly announced, "What a great honor. I am really surprised. I thought I'd have to be as old as Roy Acuff or as ugly as Willie Nelson to get in the Hall of Fame. (Just kidding Willie!)"

Amid all the accolades and honors, though, Dolly says she still feels most fulfilled with her songwriting and live performances. "Nothing beats getting out on stage and singing direct to my fans, the people who've been my friends all through the years, as well as some of the new friends I've made along the way," she says.

"NOTHING CAN TOP GETTING TO SING WITH DOLLY PARTON. NOW I CAN DIE."

– Alison Krauss

Dolly performs with Opry buddy Vince Gill on the evening of her Country Music Hall of Fame induction.

Johnny PayCheck

MORE THAN 30 YEARS

AFTER PLAYING

THE OPRY FOR THE

FIRST TIME, JOHNNY

WAS INVITED TO

OFFICIALLY JOIN THE

OPRY CAST IN 1997.

Anybody who has ever hit the alarm clock button on a work day morning knows Johnny PayCheck. His 1977 international mega hit "Take This Job and Shove It" is still the working man's anthem. The song became a million-seller, inspired a movie starring Robert Hays, and continues to be played on radio stations across the country on Friday afternoons to kick off the weekend. Johnny's career—and his life—have been about far more than that one monster smash that will live forever, however.

Born Don Eugene Lytle in Greenfield, Ohio, he was performing by age 5 and professionally by age 15. Johnny always said he was influenced by the songs of Lefty Frizell and Hank Williams, and after a stint in the Navy in the '50s he was off to play and perform the music he loved.

Johnny celebrates his Opry induction in front of a packed House.

He soon became a bass and steel guitar player in George Jones' band, where he stayed for six years. He also played with Faron Young, Porter Wagoner and Ray Price. He earned recognition as a songwriter, penning Tammy Wynette's first hit, "Apartment #9" (named an ACM Song of the Year) and Ray Price's "Touch My Heart."

In 1965 he had his first single as Johnny PayCheck. A year later he teamed up with producer Aubrey Mayhew and they started the Little Darlin' label, recording lesser known but country cult favorites on their label through the '60s.

In the '70s Johnny hit with the classic "Take This Job and Shove It" and "Don't Take Her, She's All I've Got," both of which received Grammy nominations. Other hits included "Slide off of Your Satin Sheets," "The Outlaw's Prayer," "Fifteen Beers," "Old Violin" "Mr. Lovemaker" and a duet with George Jones on "You Can Have Her."

Johnny, who always had a reputation for living the hard life of his honky tonk songs, saw his career and personal life take a downturn in the '80s, a decade which included health problems and a prison conviction.

But he was back In the '90s with a new outlook, new band, and a new look and lease on life, prompting him to advise other would-be artists, "Be prepared for a lot of hard work. Keep on the straight and narrow and don't be blinded by the excitement. Most important of all, stay away from drugs and alcohol."

Along with a new outlook came a new honor, Opry membership. More than 30 years after playing the Opry for the first time, Johnny was invited to officially join the Opry cast on November 8, 1997. Surprised with the membership invitation, Johnny said, "Yes! In a New York minute! . . . I'm so honored and proud that I'm going to be a member of the Grand Ole Opry. After a lifetime of work, this is one of the most wonderful honors bestowed on me in my entire career."

Or as Johnny might also say, take this job and love it!

Stu Phillips

Born in Montreal, Stu grew up in Calgary, Alberta, in the foothills of the Canadian Rockies, and he wrote many of his early songs in this beautiful creative setting. He grew up listening to the Grand Ole Opry on a small crystal radio set and fell in love with the Opry and country music.

Like many other members of his Opry family, Stu formed his own band at an early age and established a following playing at local events as well as working part-time for a radio station. This opened the door for a career in broadcasting. His initial job as a radio announcer led to other jobs, including producer, engineer and disc jockey.

As an on air personality, he hosted a variety of shows in Canada, including "Stu For Breakfast," "Town and Country" and "Cowtown Jamboree." From radio, Stu moved to television, first hosting a Canadian show *The Outrider*, followed by a stint on *Red River Jamboree*, a major Saturday night show on the CBC network.

In addition to his TV work, Stu began to enjoy recording success, particularly with the album *Echoes of the Canadian Foothills*. After four more years with the CBC, Stu set his sights on Music City and moved to Nashville in 1965. He got work doing a local morning TV show and that year signed with RCA Victor. With Chet Atkins as producer, Stu began hitting the country charts with tunes such as "Bracero," "The Great El Tigre," "Vin Rose," "Juanita Jones," "Note in Box #9," "The Top of the World" and "Bring Love Back Into Our World."

Opry member and new American citizen Stu Phillips is a member of the Canadian Country Music Hall of Fame.

He joined the Grand Ole Opry on June 1, 1967, after some 20 special guest appearances. "I love the Opry," Stu says. "It's tradition, a way of life for country music fans—an institution with substance and meaning for its followers. I want my career to have a similar meaning, and that means dedication and hard work."

He has toured extensively in the Far East, Middle East and Africa, where his records have received the equivalent of gold records.

In 1993 the German-based Bear Family Records released a CD featuring 35 songs from three of Stu's early albums. That same year he also released a new CD on Broadland Records, *Don't Give Up On Me*, which included the single "Rio TiaJuana," and he was inducted into the Canadian Country Music Hall of Fame. Lately his music, including the hit single "Only God," has been found at or near the top of the Christian country charts.

He still tours and performs on the Opry although he has become a minister in the Episcopal Church, receiving his divinity degree from the University of the South in Sewanee, Tennessee.

Finally, Stu Phillips, Opry member, is now Stu Phillips, American citizen. Stu, who has now lived in the U.S. longer than he lived in his native Canada, began a naturalization process in 1997 and, with wife Aldona, celebrated American citizenship on the Opry stage, Fourth of July weekend, 1998. "Our lives simply evolved over the years and took a new direction," Stu explained at the time. "Whenever I traveled overseas, I used to think of Canada as home. After moving to Nashville, our lives became integrated into this land with all its comforts. Now, whenever I travel overseas, home is Tennessee where I live."

Ray Pillow

Ray Pillow has made his mark on country music not just as a first-rate hit-maker, but also as a music publisher.

He learned to play guitar as a teen, graduated from high school, joined the Navy, and after his discharge got a degree in Business Administration from Lynchburg College.

"My first professional appearance was at the VFW Hall in Appomattox, Virginia," he recalled. "I sort of got talked into substituting for a sick member of my uncle's band. When I walked out on the stage to the microphone, I knew what I wanted to do . . . but I didn't know if I could do it. After I finished and heard the applause, I knew I was doing what I had wanted to do all along."

Ray came to Nashville in 1961 as a regional winner in the Pet Milk Talent Contest. He came in second in the national finals but his performance landed him a guest spot on the Opry and fueled his desire for a career in country music.

He released his first two singles in 1963, "Take Your Hands off my Heart" and "Thank You Ma'am." Capitol released his first album, *Presenting Ray Pillow*, in late 1965 and by 1966 he was a star. That was the year he teamed with Jean Shepard to

Ray's granddaughter Ali Ray dressed as her "Papa" when asked to dress as a famous person with the rest of her first grade class.

record two Top 10 hits—"I'll Take the Dog" and "Mr. Do-It-Yourself."

On April 30, 1966, he became a member of the Grand Ole Opry. "To be a member is like being a Phi Beta Kappa at Harvard," Ray says.

In 1967 his "Heart we did all we Could" reached the Top 14. His other chart hits include "Common Colds and Broken Hearts," "Volkswagen," "I Just Want To Be Alone," "Gone With the Wine," "Wonderful Day," "Reconsider Me," "Since Then" and "She's Doing It To Me Again."

In addition to his own music career, Ray has helped shape the professional paths of others, including Lee Greenwood. He is well known on Music Row as a publisher who can match the right artist with the right song and recording company.

Although he knew he was country, Ray has never been a "rhinestone cowboy." In fact, several record producers told him that he should be a pop singer because they said he looked like one. "But I don't want to be a pop singer," Ray says. "A country singer is all I'm ever going to be. I sing what I like to sing."

Just as he sang that night years ago in Virginia.

Charley Pride

"IT'S AS IF I HAD MADE

IT IN BASEBALL AND

THEY CAME UP TO ME

AND TOOK ME TO

COOPERSTOWN AND

SAID 'THIS IS WHERE

YOUR PLAQUE IS GOING

TO BE—BESIDE BABE

RUTH, LOU GEHRIG,

JACKIE ROBINSON AND

HANK AARON...."

Charley Pride's career really adds up. He's had 36 No. 1 hits, 30 gold and four platinum albums, and sold more than 25 million albums in his 34 years on the country music charts. He is one of the 15 all-time greatest country record sellers. And, he has countless fans.

Charley, who was born to poor sharecroppers in Sledge, Mississippi, was one of 11 children. He taught himself guitar from one he bought from Sears Roebuck when he was 14. He unofficially started his music career while a ball player in the Negro American League with the Memphis Red Sox by singing and playing guitar on the team bus between ballparks.

It was while he was playing for Memphis that he met his wife Rozene. They have been married for more than 40 years and have two sons, Kraig and Dion, and a daughter, Angela.

After a tryout with the New York Mets, Charley decided to return home via Nashville. It was there that he met manager Jack Johnson, who, upon hearing the singer, sent him back home with a promise that a contract would follow.

A year later Charley was back in Nashville and introduced to producer Jack Clement. After hearing Charley's rendition of several songs he had asked him to learn, Clement asked Charley if he could cut two songs in two hours. Charley agreed, and "Snakes Crawl At Night" and "The Atlantic Coastal Line" were recorded.

"Snakes Crawl at Night" was a hit, but nobody had seen photos of the singer. Charley made a public appearance in support of the single at a show in Detroit

hosted by Ralph Emery. When he stepped on stage the loud applause got lower and lower to dead silence as the audience realized Charley was an African American country singer. Race didn't matter, however. By the end of the night, he was besieged with autograph seekers and the rest, as they say, is history.

Charley's songs have become classics— "Kiss An Angel Good Morning" (a crossover million-seller), "I'm So Afraid of Losing You Again," "Mountain of Love," "Is Anybody Going To San Antone?" and "All I Have to Offer You Is Me."

With the hits came awards by the armful. In 1971 he was named CMA Entertainer of the Year. That year, and the next, he was also CMA Male Vocalist of the Year and he picked up three Grammys. In 1980, *Cash Box* magazine named him the Top Male Country Artist of the '70s, and in 1994 the Academy of Country Music gave him the prestigious Pioneer Award.

On May 1, 1993, 26 years after he first played there as a guest, Charley joined the Grand Ole Opry. Remembering his initial dream of baseball stardom, Charley said, "It's as if I had made it in baseball and they came up to me and took me to Cooperstown and said 'This is where your plaque is going to be—beside Babe Ruth, Lou Gehrig, Jackie Robinson and Hank Aaron...." Opry membership to Charley means "thinking about the tradition of growing up and listening to all of those people and now here I am a member of that elite group."

Recognized as one of country music's all-time top acts, Charley visits backstage with fellow Opry members Jim Ed Brown and Patty Loveless.

Jeanne Pruett

Visit the Grand Ole Opry any season of the year and you'll likely hear Jeanne Pruett introduced as "Miss Satin Sheets." While Jeanne has enjoyed worldwide success with dozens of singles, it was, indeed, "Satin Sheets" that earned 1973 Song, Single and Album of the Year nominations from the Country Music Association. The song also led to a Female Vocalist of the Year nomination that same year. Twelve months later, Jeanne walked away with Female Album and Album of the Year honors from *Billboard* magazine.

Jeanne was born in Pell City, Alabama—one of 10 children—to a full-time farmer and part-time cotton mill worker. Both parents had a great love of music and a great appreciation for Jeanne's talent.

Jeanne spent her young years singing whenever and wherever she could. She moved to Nashville in 1956 and started her Music Row career as a songwriter with Marty Robbins Enterprises. She wrote many hits for Marty, including "Count Me Out," "Waiting in Reno," "Lily of the Valley" and "Love Me." Years later, Jeanne lists "the many Saturday night 11:30 p.m. shows I shared the stage with my late, great friend Marty Robbins" as some of the most memorable moments of her Opry career.

Her songs have also been recorded by Tammy Wynette, Nat Stuckey, Conway Twitty and others, and Jeanne always says "It is easier to be accepted in the music business by your peers as a performer after you have proven yourself as a writer. The acceptance of the fans is another thing. You sell them after you have gone into the studio and come up with the best you have."

She won their acceptance in 1971 with her first hit, "Hold to my Unchanging Love," which she followed with "Love Me."

But they just set the stage for what was to come. "Satin Sheets" hit country radio in 1973 and on July 21 of that year Jeanne became an official member of the Opry. "I had been a member for months, but I didn't know it until Porter and Dolly called me out to sing and announced it. . . . Shock City!" Jeanne recalls.

"Satin Sheets" made her an international star and she was voted 1974's Best Female Artist by England's *Music Week Magazine*.

She had more hits in the '70s including "I'm Your Woman," "You Don't Need to Move a Mountain," "Welcome to the Sunshine (Sweet Baby Jane)," "Just Like Your Daddy," "A Poor Man's Woman," "I'm Living a Lie" and "Please Sing Satin Sheets For Me." In the '80s she hit again with three major hits in one year. "Back To Back," "Temporarily Yours" and "It's Too Late."

In recent years she has been a hit with something other than music—but something near and dear to her heart—cooking. She is the author, editor and publisher of four best-selling cookbooks called *Feedin' Friends*.

Jeanne says her fans might be surprised that, yes, she loves to do just that: "I still do a lot of home canning such as tomatoes, preserves and love it!"

Jeanne, the girl from the Alabama farm, is back on the farm. She and husband Eddie Fulton have a 160-acre ranch and farm outside Nashville. But on sunny days, you might also find Jeanne on nearby Center Hill Lake aboard her 65-foot houseboat. Not unlike its owner, the craft has been dubbed "Miss Satin Sheets."

Jeanne has friends in Opry places! Miss Satin Sheets greets Garth Brooks backstage.

Del Reeves

Del Reeves has been playing country classics for more than 30 years.

AFTER PORTER WAGONER

INTRODUCED HIM AS THE

LATEST MEMBER OF THE

GRAND OLE OPRY, DEL

BURST INTO TEARS AND

COULD ONLY SING THE

CHORUS AND END OF

HIS SONG."

Friend and fellow songwriter Hank Cochran talked Del Reeves into moving to Nashville from California in 1962. After nine No. 1 hits, Del's still here, still performing—singer, actor, stand-up comic, impressionist and one of the greatest stage performers in country music history.

As Mel Tillis says, "He's fan-t-t-tastic."

Born Franklin Delano Reeves in Sparta, North Carolina, the youngest of 11 children, he was playing a regular gig on a local Saturday radio show by age 12. As Del tells it, "I had four brothers in World War II and when they left home they left their old guitars laying around. I got to playing around with them, and little by little, learned to play. My mother used to tune the guitar for me."

Del attended Appalachia State College in Boone, North Carolina, and then served four years in the Air Force. While stationed at Travis Air Force Base in California he began writing songs, singing on country music television shows and recording with Capitol Records. After his military discharge, he stayed in California where he was building a strong reputation as a singer-songwriter-performer with songs recorded by Carl Smith and Roy Drusky.

He moved to Music City in 1962 and in 1965 his United Artists million-selling recording of "The Girl On the Billboard" went to No. 1. That same year, "The Belles of Southern Bell" went Top 5. In 1966, "Women Do Funny Things To Me" hit Top 10, and Del hit the Opry stage as a full-fledged member on October 14. After Porter Wagoner introduced him as the latest member of the Grand Ole Opry, Del—whose parents were in the audience to witness the night's events—burst into tears and could only sing the chorus and end of his song.

Other smash records include "Philadelphia Phillies," "Take me to Your Heart," "Swinging Doors" and "Slow Hand." He has had more than 25 hit songs.

The tall, thin performer has appeared in eight movies including the 1969 film *Sam Whiskey* with Burt Reynolds, Angie Dickinson and Clint Walker. He also hosted his own television Show, *Del Reeves Country Carnival.*

These days Del can be found on the Opry stage pleasing audiences with one of his signature hits or one of his engaging impersonations of any number of other country acts. Off stage, Del leads a quiet rural life with his wife and family raising horses and cattle.

Riders In The Sky

IT'S THE TIME YOU

TAKE IN SMELLING ALL

THE ROSES ON THE WAY.

IT'S DOING JUST

THE BEST YOU CAN,

IT'S THE COWBOY WAY.

When you hear that "Great Big Western Howdy" you know it's time to saddle up for those American icons of the great cowboy songs, the western trio Riders In The Sky featuring the talents of Ranger Doug (the idol of American youth), Woody Paul and Too Slim.

For more than 20 years these madcap cowpokes have been bringing their flawless instrumentation and harmony to audiences, serving up a heapin' helpin' of Western songs and impeccable humor to fans around the globe.

The three saddle pals got their start in 1977 at a Nashville nightclub called Phranks and Steins. What they had in common was living in the same Nashville neighborhood and a love of authentic Western cowboy songs. They practiced in each other's living rooms, took their name from an old Sons of the Pioneers album cover, got their wives to whip out some wonderful western wear on their Singers and hit the road in an old GMC van with a saddle for a front seat, and stage props that included an electric campfire and a 200-pound saguaro cactus.

They released their first album, *Three On The Trail*, in 1980 and performed at President Reagan's inaugural ball. A year later they were inducted into the Country Music Foundation's Walkway of Stars. They

The Riders on location at the Toy Story 2 music video shoot. (Photo Mark Lowrie)

sang in *Sweet Dreams*, Jessica Lange's film biography of Patsy Cline, and became members of the Opry on June 19, 1982. Among other Riders' career highs: the group created its own *Tumbleweed* series on TNN, *Riders Radio Theatre* for National Public Radio, made a jingle for Levi's jeans, performed with heroes Roy Rogers and Gene Autry and even taught Barney the purple dinosaur to yodel.

The group has logged more than two million miles, performed 4,000 live shows singing 65,000 songs, made nearly 200 national television appearances and released 21 albums—including its latest releases *Public Cowboy #1: The Music of Gene Autry* and *A Great Big Western Howdy*. The only trail riding the Riders do is 200 concert dates a year—lately with sidekick Joey the Cowpolka King on accordion.

"As we look back it has been an incredible 20 years," says Ranger Doug. "We never set out to do this. It was just three guys out there singing songs they liked and having fun. We took a style of music that was so far in the past that it became fresh again because people hadn't heard it in years." They couldn't be happier with their songs and success—even without the platinum albums or big country music awards. As they told *Country Music* magazine recently, "We've always had a great time and we believe in what we are doing. So we keep boogieing down the road playing cowboy music."

Johnny Russell

"Can everybody see me alright?"

It's a phrase Opry fans have come to expect to hear when the big red curtain goes up for another performance from singer/song-writer/comedian Johnny Russell. The big fellow with the big, big hits has earned a reputation for having fun with the guests on his Opry segments as well as for poking fun at himself.

"This next song was written by one of my favorite songwriters . . . me!" Johnny often laughs before kicking off one of his many self-penned tunes. He began writing songs at an early age. Jim Reeves put his "In A Mansion Stands My Love" on the B side of his No. 1 country hit of 1959, "He'll Have to Go." And Johnny likes to tell his audiences how he has collected royalties from a million-seller that few people remember.

Johnny had the last laugh with one of his most recorded songs ever. He tried unsuccessfully to get it cut for more than two years. The song? "Act Naturally," which, of course became a country standard after its release by Buck Owens and after it was also recorded by Ringo Starr. In 1989, Owens and Starr re-worked the song as a duo and filmed an accompanying video.

Good times! John Berry and Johnny share a laugh on the Opry stage.

Johnny's songs have been recorded by countless other music greats including Burl Ives, George Strait, Bobby Vinton, Patti Page and Gene Watson as well as fellow Opry members George Jones, Loretta Lynn, Dolly Parton and Del Reeves.

The Opry member since July 6, 1985, also has recorded hits of his own. In 1971, he moved to Nashville to pursue a recording career to compliment his successful songwriting stint. Country Music Hall of Famer Chet Atkins signed the singer to a RCA recording contract and, 30 years later, remains impressed with Johnny's vocal style. "I think if you could find the definition of country music in Webster's Dictionary," Atkins says, "You would surely see songs like 'Rednecks, White Socks and Blue-Ribbon Beer,' 'Catfish John' and 'The Baptism of Jesse Taylor'" as some of the finest examples of that definition."

Johnny also enjoyed success with "Mr. And Mrs. Untrue," "Rain Falling on Me," "Hello I Love You," "Ain't No Way to Make A Bad Love Grow" and "Song of the South."

In addition to regular Opry appearances, Johnny has become a fan favorite recently at bluegrass festivals across the region. Fans can always catch him performing at the annual Johnny Russell Day in his hometown of Moorhead, Mississippi. Proceeds from the annual event, which started in 1988, go to the Johnny Russell Scholarship fund at Mississippi Delta Junior College.

Jeannie Seely

JEANNIE, WHO WAS

RAISED IN TOWNVILLE,

PENNSYLVANIA,

REMEMBERS SITTING

IN THE FAMILY'S FORD,

EATING POPCORN AND

DRINKING SODA POP,

LISTENING TO

THE GRAND OLE OPRY

ON SATURDAY NIGHTS

WHILE HER PARENTS

PLAYED CARDS

AT FRIENDS' HOUSES.

Jeannie Seely knew at age 4 what she wanted to be.

Her mother said that was the age when she would stretch to reach the knob on her family's big console radio, find 650 WSM on the dial and keep it there. Jeannie is still on the dial at 650 WSM—performing regularly on the stage of the Opry.

Jeannie, who was raised in Townville, Pennsylvania, remembers sitting in the family's Ford, eating popcorn and drinking soda pop, listening to the Grand Ole Opry on Saturday nights while her parents played cards at friends' houses.

By age 11, she was performing on a weekly radio show in Meadville, Pennsylvania.

Years of playing auditoriums, small clubs, and country music parks followed. She also had a two-year-stint as a disc jockey on her own Armed Forces Network show and followed that as a secretary with Liberty and Imperial Records in Hollywood before moving to Nashville at the urging of late Opry member Dottie West in 1965. "I don't know enough to go there yet," Jeannie remembers saying to her dear friend. Dottie's response: "Jeannie, that's where you go to learn."

A recording contract with Monument Records gave her the first hit in 1966,

Jeannie sings of a "Winter Wonderland" during the Opry's Holiday Season.

"Don't Touch Me." It went to No. 1 and won her the 1966 Grammy for Best Female Country Vocal Performance.

One year later on September 16, 1967, she fulfilled a childhood dream by becoming a member of the Opry cast.

Other hits followed—"Can I Sleep in Your Arms," "Lucky Ladies," "Little Things," "Tell Me Again," "I'll Love You More" and "Please Be my New Love." Jeannie is also a successful songwriter —having had songs recorded by good friend Dottie West, Faron Young, Connie Smith, Willie Nelson, Ray Price and others.

Jeannie's latest projects include the CD *Been There . . . Sung That* which features country standards as well as vocal collaborations with friends Willie Nelson and T. Graham Brown. She's also made recent Opryland holiday seasons more memorable with her Holiday Breakfast and Music Celebration during the Opryland Hotel's Country Christmas Celebration.

In 2000, she hit the road for Atlantic City to portray the character of Louise opposite friend Terri Williams in *Always . . . Patsy Cline*. The role was that of an energetic, funny woman with a heart full of love for her friends and for country music. Can you say "perfect casting?"

Ricky Van Shelton

Ricky Van Shelton is one of those overnight country music successes that was years in the making.

Ricky's title track from his debut album *Wild Eyed Dream* hit the Top 10 in 1987 and began a streak of 13 No. 1 hits. But Ricky had worked years as a salesman, house painter, plumber, appliance store manager and construction worker—working days and practicing at night waiting for that big break.

Ricky was brought up in the tiny community of Grit, Virginia, where his family still lives today. He was the youngest of five children, all of whom loved the outdoors and spent lots of time hiking and camping.

He added his middle name Van to avoid being confused with another Ricky Shelton in his hometown.

In high school he was recognized as an exceptional artist and singer. Young Ricky took art classes and was in the chorus. After high school he continued performing locally.

In 1984, he moved to Nashville with his wife Bettye and worked various day jobs while practicing his music.

In June 1986, he was offered a recording contract with CBS Records. One year later he had his first Top 10 hit. On June 10, 1988, he became a member of the Grand Ole Opry telling his audience that he had dreamed of having a big bus and hearing himself on the radio. "And I dreamed about playing on the Grand Ole Opry," Ricky told the audience, "but one thing I never dreamed is that I'd be asked to join."

From his first recording, country fans realized that they were witnessing the rise of an especially gifted singer who performed in the smooth style of Eddy Arnold, Jim Reeves and Conway Twitty.

His steady stream of No. 1 hits include "Somebody Lied," "I'll Leave This World Loving You," "I Am a Simple Man," "Keep it Between the Lines," "I've Cried My Last Tear for You," "Statue of a Fool," "From a Jack to a King," "Living Proof," "Life Turned Her That Way" and "Don't We All Have the Right." In 1991 he teamed with Dolly Parton for the smash hit duet "Rockin' Years."

Today Ricky keeps a busy concert and recording schedule. He has also distinguished himself as a painter, author, pilot and collector.

His series of children's books *Tales from a Duck Named Quacker* has sold more than 200,000 copies and his paintings can be viewed by his fans on the Internet.

Ricky chats with Jim Ed Brown before delivering "Statue of a Fool."

Jean Shepard

Jean Shepard was the first country female vocalist in the post-war era to sell a million records. She was the first to overdub her voice on record and the first to make a color television commercial. She was also the first singing female Opry member to celebrate 40 years with the Opry cast. And she'll be the last to sing anything but that upon which she's built her enduring career—*pure country*—emphasis on both words.

Jean was born in Oklahoma but grew up in Visalia, California, one of 10 children who were all musically inclined. When she was 14 she formed an all-girl western swing band called "The Melody Ranch Girls." Soon they were playing dances and local radio shows.

Jean treats the Opry audience to a country classic.

One night "The Melody Ranch Girls" played a show with country legend Hank Thompson. He was so impressed with Jean that he introduced her to record executives and set up a recording deal with Capitol Records. She cut her first record when she was only 15.

Jean soon moved to Springfield, Missouri, to join Red Foley and the stars on the Ozark Jubilee. Next she enjoyed monster success with Ferlin Husky on the "Dear John Letter" and its sequel "Forgive Me John." Both records sold more than a million copies, and she and Ferlin played to crowds throughout the U.S. Jean then took her distinct country stylings to the Grand Ole Opry, earning Opry membership on November 21, 1955.

She has recorded more than 25 albums—including the 1956 *Songs of a Love Affair* on which she wrote all 12 songs—and has hit the charts with releases such as "Satisfied Mind," "Another Lonely Night," "Then He Touched Me," "Seven Lonely Days," "Slipping Away," "At the Time," "I'll Do Anything" and "Tips of my Fingers."

Jean married Opry great Hawkshaw Hawkins and had a son Don Robin, named for their good friends Don Gibson and Marty Robbins. In March 1963 she was eight months pregnant with their second child when Hawkshaw died in the tragic plane crash that also took the lives of Opry stars Cowboy Copas and Patsy Cline and Patsy's manager and pilot Randy Hughes. When Jean's son was born a month later, she named him Harold Franklin Hawkins II for his father.

Jean today is happily married to Benny Birchfield, a musician, singer and member of Nashville's music community. Together with their versatile band "The Second Fiddles" they tour extensively throughout the U.S., Canada and Europe entertaining audiences with *pure country*—emphasis on both words.

Ricky Skaggs

It takes a lot of talent to be called a "recognized master" of one of America's most demanding art forms by age 21. But it takes even more to build that early success into a decades-long career of artistic success and public acclaim. That's been the story of Ricky Skaggs, and now he's bringing that talent and reputation back to where it all began— bluegrass music.

Born on July 18, 1954, in Eastern Kentucky, Ricky was already an accomplished singer and mandolin player by the time he reached his teens. He entered the world of professional music with his friend, late country singer Keith Whitley. The two young musicians were taken under the wing of bluegrass pioneer Ralph Stanley in 1971. Short but significant periods with other top acts came next. Ricky began to build a reputation for creativity and excitement through live appearances and recordings with such acts as J.D. Crowe & The New South. He performed on the group's 1975 debut for Rounder Records, which was widely acknowledged as one of the most influential bluegrass albums ever made. A stint as a bandleader with Boone Creek followed, bringing the challenges of leadership while giving him further recording and performing experience.

Beginning in the late 1970s, Ricky turned his attention to country music. Though still in his 20s, the wealth of experience and talent he possessed served him well, first as a member of Emmylou Harris' Hot Band, and then on his own. With the release of *Waitin' For The Sun To Shine* in 1981, Ricky moved to the top of the country charts. He remained there through most of the 1980s—long enough to earn a spot in *Billboard's* Top 20 artists of the decade and Top 100 of the past 50 years. Ricky's popularity (24 singles in *Billboard's* Top 20, including 12 No. 1s) was matched by his esteem among critics and fellow musicians. The result: eight awards from the Country Music Association, including Entertainer Of The Year in 1985, Grammys and dozens of other honors. Indeed, renowned guitarist and producer Chet Atkins credited Ricky with "single-handedly saving country music."

Ricky joined the Grand Ole Opry family May 15, 1982.

With exposure spanning from Opry appearances to broadcasting on the Internet, Ricky has since become one of bluegrass' most personable and effective ambassadors.

At the center of Ricky's emergence as a bluegrass leader was his Grammy-winning album *Bluegrass Rules!*. A true labor of love, it joined Ricky's roots and experience with classic material from the first generation of bluegrass masters. It also put the music in the hands of a carefully assembled team that shared his delight in creating a sound at once familiar and excitingly new.

The most recent testament of Ricky's ability to compete in the bluegrass arena is his 2000 Grammy Award for Best Bluegrass Album for *Ancient Tones*. The bluegrass aficionado's most recent releases are his first gospel release *Soldier of the Cross* and a tribute album to bluegrass and Opry legend Bill Monroe.

Ricky Skaggs had the honor of inviting Trisha Yearwood to become a member of the Opry cast.

Melvin Sloan Dancers

For almost 50 years the Sloan Dancers have been exciting Opry audiences with their unique Appalachian-style square dancing.

Ralph Sloan and his dancers, "The Tennessee Travelers," first appeared on the Opry in 1952. After Ralph's death in 1980, his brother Melvin took over the reins. Through the span of six decades, the Sloan Brothers' dedication has been such that the dancers have never missed a scheduled Opry performance.

The Sloan Dancers perform the unique style that is a part of middle Tennessee heritage. Each dancer interprets the music with his or her own style and steps as Melvin calls out various dance patterns. Team members are natives of the area and have the God-given talent of rhythm and coordination that allows them to execute the intricate steps and patterns with showmanship.

No other square dance group in the world has reached the level of achievement that the Sloan Dancers have. The group's credits include thousands of Grand Ole Opry performances, hundreds of television appearances and festivals across the country.

Recognition of the group's contributions to middle Tennessee culture have come from a variety of distinguished persons and

Dance break. Melvin and Wylie Gustafson (lead singer of Wylie & the Wild West) talk offstage.

organizations. In 1980, the Tennessee State Legislature recognized the group's Appalachian-style square dancing by designating it as the state dance and named Ralph Sloan as Ambassador of Southern Appalachian Square Dancing.

The Melvin Sloan Dancers were invited by then-President Ronald Reagan to perform at the John F. Kennedy Center for the Performing Arts in Washington, D.C., during a tribute to the "King of Country Music" Roy Acuff.

The Country Music Foundation recognized Ralph's contribution to the Country Music industry by inducting him in the Walkway of Stars at the Country Music Hall of Fame in Nashville. Brother Melvin presented Ralph's dancing shoes and costume along with a copy of the book *An Overview of Square Dancing at the Grand Ole Opry* in a special ceremony conducted at the Hall of Fame.

In 1997 Ralph and Melvin Sloan were inducted into America's Clogging Hall of Fame in Maggie Valley, North Carolina. This prestigious award recognized their contributions in promoting and preserving the art of Southern Appalachian Square Dancing.

Thus the tradition of Sloan Square Dancing continues. Now, as in the past, these unequaled dancers eagerly await the music to begin, the curtain to rise and the bright lights to flood the stage so that once again they can demonstrate to the world their love of square dancing.

Connie Smith

There's really only three female singers in the world: Streisand, Ronstadt and Connie Smith. The rest of us are only pretending.

—Dolly Parton

Big words from a woman who, herself, is heralded as having one of country music's all-time best voices. But countless others agree with Dolly.

Connie was born Constance Meador in Elkhart, Indiana, and grew up in Hinton, West Virginia. She was a bashful little girl in a family of 14, but Connie says she remembers saying at age 5, "Someday I'm gonna sing on the Grand Ole Opry."

She was a housewife and mother of a four-month-old son in Warner, Ohio, in 1963 when she and her husband made a trip to Columbus to see Opry star Bill Anderson perform at the Frontier Ranch Park. She got talked into entering a talent contest, subsequently won, and got to meet Bill. He offered to help her launch a country music career.

She first visited Nashville in March 1964 to appear on the Ernest Tubb Record Shop radio show. Bill had invited her and was supposed to host the show, but in the end, Ernest hosted the show himself.

Opry legend Connie Smith greets successful new group SHeDAISY backstage before the group's Opry debut.

Connie sang a Bill Anderson song and received countless compliments, one of them from Loretta Lynn.

Although he had missed hearing her sing, Bill Anderson invited her back in May to do some demonstration records. The following month Chet Atkins signed her to RCA Records and in July she recorded a song written by Bill, "Once A Day." It was released in August. By November it was at No. 1, where it stayed for more than two months. Her first album spent 30 weeks on the charts, including seven at No. 1.

The hits continued: "Then and Only Then," "I Can't Remember," "If I Talk to Him," "Nobody Lovin'" and "The Hurtin's all Over" —all in 1965. Connie joined the Opry family on June 13 during that hit-filled year as well. The next year she followed with "I'll Come Runnin'" and "Burning a Hole in my Mind." Then "Baby's Back Again" and "Run Away with Tears" in 1968.

By that time Connie was ready to run away from the hassles and pressures of constant touring, movies and recording. Her family, not her career, was her priority. She took time off to concentrate on her five children and her church. She rejoined the Opry in 1971.

Today her kids are grown and she's back writing and working with Nashville's finest —Harlan Howard and Allen Shamblin among them. She recently released her first studio album in 20 years, simply titled *Connie Smith*. Of course Opry fans know that another one of her co-writers on the project is not only a fellow Opry member, but also her husband, Marty Stuart. "I think Marty and I match so well," Connie has said. "I love him with all my heart."

Dolly Parton and countless others would say that, so too, are Connie and country music a "perfect match." And they love her with all their hearts.

Mike Snider

"Boy, this feels like home," Mike Snider thought the first time he walked on the stage of the Opry for a guest appearance. The fact that there were 2,000 people from his hometown in the audience cheering him on and giving him four standing ovations likely contributed to the feeling.

Six years later on June 2, 1990, Mike was officially home as he joined the Opry family with the Queen of Country Comedy Minnie Pearl calling him one of her "dear, dear, friends." Mike learned about the Opry lying on the floor and watching it on television. "I never thought about getting on it, let alone be a member of it," he says.

He got his first banjo on his 16th birthday after hearing a Flatt and Scruggs album. He soon became the Tennessee State Bluegrass Banjo Champion and won the Mid-South Banjo Playing Contest. At age 23, just six years after getting his first banjo, he won the National Bluegrass Banjo Championship.

Soon his banjo, fiddle, and harmonica playing coupled with his down-home way of talking had launched him as a real country picker and comedian.

Mike, his wife Sweetie and the kids. Mike says, "I've been married to the same woman for 17 years. . . . You can tell I ain't no real country star!"

Mike says that it took folks a while to realize that his genuine accent was not an intended comedy routine." People started laughing at my accent, but I wasn't trying to be funny," he said. Today, he does try to be funny . . . and succeeds when referring to another "sitting ovation" or when delivering the lyrics of songs such as "The Fur Coat" and "Born to Shop."

Add his instrumental work as well as that of his band that consists of Blake Williams, Bobby Clark and Charlie Cushman, and Opry audiences never really know what to expect.

Mike's latest projects include three CDs: "*Mike Snider–Comedy Songs,*" "*Mike Snider–Old Time Favorites*" and "*Mike Snider– Gospel Harmonica.*"

He, his wife Sabrina—known to his fans as "Sweetie"—and their children Katie Lynn and Blake still call Gleason, Tennessee, their home.

Ralph Stanley

Throughout his career that has spanned more than 50 years, Ralph Stanley has influenced artists from Bob Dylan to Dolly Parton and has been a mentor for Ricky Skaggs, Larry Sparks, Charlie Sizemore and the late Keith Whitley, all past members of his band The Clinch Mountain Boys.

Born February 25, 1927, in the Clinch Mountains of Dickenson County, Virginia, he learned to play the banjo from his mother Lucy. In 1946, he and his brother Carter formed the Stanley Brothers, and their unique blend of religious music, bluegrass and "square dance" licks is still present in Stanley's music today.

The Stanley Brothers began their career at WCYB in Bristol, Virginia, where they worked for 12 years. An association with Jim Walter took them to Florida where they were broadcast in Tallahassee and Orlando and appeared on a 30-minute television program transmitted throughout the south.

Tragedy struck in 1966 when Carter passed away from cancer. However, support from friends and fans encouraged Ralph to continue the tradition of the Stanley Brothers.

Stanley has recorded more than 150 solo projects including *Classic Gospel Ralph Stanley, Ralph Stanley 50th Anniversary Collection, Clinch Mountain Gospel* and *Classic Stanley* with Roy Lee Centers, Keith Whitley and Ricky Skaggs, to name a few.

The sign says it all. Patty Loveless and Chet Atkins congratulate Ralph on his Opry induction.

One of Ralph's latest endeavors is a one-of-a-kind project titled *Clinch Mountain Country* which includes collaborations with 34 artists such as Ricky Skaggs, Joe Diffie, Hal Ketchum, Jim Lauderdale, Alison Krauss, Connie Smith, Bob Dylan, Gillian Welch, Vince Gill and countless others. Hal Ketchum stated that "Singing with Ralph Stanley is like painting with Picasso."

The Stanley Brothers were inducted into the International Bluegrass Music Association's Hall of Honor in 1992. Ralph has received accolades for his work from countless music associations including the IBMA and NARAS.

On January 15, 2000, Ralph celebrated another career milestone when he was inducted as a member of the Grand Ole Opry by longtime musical friends Patty Loveless and Porter Wagoner. Patty says of her friend and fellow Opry member, "There is a specialness to his music, a magic to the music he makes . . . I think it will live on for many generations to come."

It is difficult to describe the influence that Ralph Stanley has had on the world of music. It is even more difficult, perhaps, to condense into a few sentences what it is that makes his voice and music so special and unique. Country music star Junior Brown's description, however, comes as close as anyone could hope. "His voice has a lot of character, a lot of personality," observes Junior. "It's what country music, bluegrass music, whatever you want to call it, is supposed to be about. Not about hot licks, not about fancy songs and this and that. It is about that feeling you can hear when Ralph sings. When I hear Ralph's boys and his banjo, it reminds me of what music is supposed to be all about."

Marty Stuart

Singer. Songwriter. Poet. Musician. Photographer. Movie score composer. Historian. Collector. Actor. Comic book hero. Marty Stuart is "Country Music's Renaissance Man."

He may be as progressive as any artist out there, but his country roots run deep and wide. He made his first appearance on the Opry as a 13-year-old mandolin-playing teen-ager traveling with Lester Flatt's band. After Lester died in 1979, Marty branched out playing a kind of bluegrass fusion with fiddle player Vassar Clements and working with guitar virtuoso Doc Watson.

A six-year stint touring with Johnny Cash followed and Marty, who plays guitar, bass, mandolin and fiddle, became a sought-after sessions and concert musician playing with Willie Nelson, Emmylou Harris, Bob Dylan, Randy Travis and even Roy Rogers.

He signed with MCA Records in 1989, breaking the Top 10 for the first time in 1990 with the album *Hillbilly Rock*, which went gold. His second album *Tempted* also went gold with four hits: "Tempted," "Little Things," "Till I Found You" and "Burn Me Down."

He wrote two songs that became award-winning duets with his "no hats" friend Travis Tritt. The pair's collaboration on "The Whiskey Ain't Workin'" and "This One's Gonna Hurt You" brought the team a Country Music Association Award for Vocal Event of the Year (1992) and "Whiskey" won a Grammy (1993). On November 28, 1992, Marty became a member of the Grand Ole Opry, 20 years after his first appearance at age 13.

Marty's singles, albums and work with other artists on tribute albums bring together a vast array of music styles—honky tonk, hillbilly, rock, traditional country, progressive —in a way that brings out the best of all styles. As he says, "It's just about being fearless and having fun. It's like somebody said to me, 'You sounded like you grew up, but you got over it.'" Marty has also assembled one of the largest collections of country music memorabilia, including the Country Music Hall of Fame Hank Williams Exhibit, and is known round the world for his contribution to country music. He has served as Ambassador of Tourism for the City of Nashville and President of the Country Music Foundation.

Recently Marty scored and produced the music for the Billy Bob Thornton movie *Daddy and Them* and the soundtrack album with Dwight Yoakam and Sheryl Crow.

He has been honored by Martin Guitar with a limited edition signature series acoustic guitar and by Fender Guitars with a signature series Fender Telecaster.

But Marty doesn't just sing, write, play and perform the country and bluegrass he loves so much. He photographs the people, the places, and the performers with the same soul he gives his songs. He has had photos published in *Country Music*, *People* and *Southern Living* magazines and a Cheekwood Gallery (Nashville) showing. His book *Pilgrims: Sinners, Saints & Prophets*, featuring essays and photos of country greats—everybody from Earl Scruggs to Jerry Lee Lewis—captures the essence and soul of country.

Marty Stuart: renaissance man—and heart and soul man—of country music.

A stage of legends. Marty jams with Hall of Famer Earl Scruggs and American icon Andy Griffith.

Randy Travis

When Randy Travis hit Nashville, it was deep in its "Urban Cowboy," pop-country phase. Randy was intent on bringing back its fiddles, steel guitars and honky-tonk lyrics.

He had recorded for a tiny label, and, in classic country fashion, drove from radio station to radio station throughout the South to promote his work. After five years of paying dues in North Carolina, he and manager Lib Hatcher moved to Music City with little more than dreams and determination to sustain them. Back then, not a single executive on Music Row could hear the possibilities in Randy's warm, subtly shaded backwoods baritone. He was turned down by every record label in town.

Lib took a job managing a night club near the Grand Ole Opry House called the Nashville Palace. Randy became its dishwasher and short-order cook. Occasionally, he'd take off his grease-stained apron and emerge from the kitchen to sing a song, which would invariably make the hard-core country patrons go wild.

Finally, Lib was able to secure Randy a deal with Warner Brothers Records. In 1985, the label released the single "On The Other Hand" with little response. Randy's second single, "1982," though, really kicked his career into high gear. George Jones, Loretta Lynn and other Opry cast members and country legends voiced their support for the plain-spoken young man from North Carolina— they had found someone to "carry the torch" into the future.

Randy's major label debut album *Storms of Life* appeared in 1986 and went on to sell more than four million copies. *Always and Forever*, his second collection, was No. 1 for 10 solid months and won a Grammy. *Old 8x10*, his third set, also won a Grammy. To be sure, the first boom in the "new country" movement had sounded. By the time Randy turned 30, he'd sold more than 13 million albums thanks to radio hits such as "Forever And Ever, Amen," "Diggin' up Bones," "Deeper Than the Holler," "Hard Rock Bottom of Your Heart," "He Walked on Water" and others.

With the hits came rooms full of awards. When the Academy of Country Music named him Top New Male Vocalist and the CMA bestowed its prestigious Horizon Award, it was just the beginning. Male Vocalist, Single, Song, Album and Entertainer of the Year honors from the top industry and fan associations followed. On December 20, 1986, Randy became a member of the Grand Ole Opry, an honor he ranked at the time as special as his platinum albums and the opportunity to record with one of his heroes George Jones. Not long thereafter, his manager became his manager/wife.

While Randy continues to record and chart hit records, he's also caught the acting bug in recent years, appearing in nearly 20 TV movies and a dozen feature films.

Randy strums his guitar while relaxing in style.

Travis Tritt

Travis Tritt mixed the rowdiness of Southern rock with the traditional honky-tonk laments and came up with a sound that rocked the country music world beginning with his first release "Country Club" in 1989.

"I'm a firm believer that there's only two kinds of music—good and bad," Travis says. "I like to describe my music as a triangle. On one side is a folk influence from people like James Taylor, Larry Gatlin and John Denver. On the second side is George Jones and Merle Haggard—that type of music. And then on the third side is The Allman Brothers and The Marshall Tucker Band. They're all balanced together, all part of what I do."

It was in Marietta, Georgia, that Travis began his musical career as a soloist in his church's children's choir. He taught himself guitar at age 8 and wrote his first song at age 14. For many years he worked as a solo artist on the Atlanta club circuit before coming to Nashville.

A local representative of Warner Bros. Records helped him produce demo tapes that led to the label signing him in 1988. His album *Country Club* gave us three No. 1 singles: "Help Me Hold On," "I'm Gonna Be Somebody" and "Drift off to Dream." The title cut was a Top 10 hit in 1989 and *Billboard* named him Top New Male Artist in 1990.

In 1991 he came back with another album of hits, seven of the 10 cuts self-penned. *It's All About To Change* yielded three more No. 1 songs, including the famed "Here's A Quarter (Call Someone Who Cares)."

That same year the Country Music Association gave him the Horizon Award. Next up was Opry membership on February 29, 1992. Membership was a bit of a surprise, Travis revealed, saying, "All my life I've dreamed about this. At one point I didn't know if I would ever be invited to be on the Opry because I have a side that's a little more contemporary. But I'm a country artist. I've always been and it's a privilege to be here."

His hit "The Whiskey Ain't Workin'" paired him with Opry buddy Marty Stuart, and the duo took home a CMA award later in 1992 and a Grammy in 1993.

He showed a half-billion people just what a dynamic entertainer he is when he performed during half-time at the 1993 Super Bowl, and in 1994 his *Ten Feet Tall and Bulletproof* autobiography was published.

In addition to continued hit albums and acting credits in recent years, Travis took on other important roles—husband and father. While his songs may portray the image of a rowdy honky-tonker, Travis says he is quite the family man. He's one of many country acts who have taken extended breaks from recording and touring to spend time with his family.

Recently, Travis signed a new record deal with Sony Nashville, allowing him to continue putting out the kind of music that has made Travis the unique musical stylist that he is.

TRAVIS BEGAN HIS MUSICAL CAREER AS A SOLOIST IN HIS CHURCH'S CHILDREN'S CHOIR

Travis Tritt surprises Opry buddy Marty Stuart for an Opry jam.

Porter Wagoner

HIS FLASHY SUITS,

SENSE OF HUMOR, AND

STAGE PRESENCE HAVE

MADE HIM ONE OF THE

MOST RECOGNIZED

FIGURES IN COUNTRY

MUSIC TODAY.

Porter Wagoner—the Wagonmaster—the thin man from West Plains with the spangled suits has been recording hits since the early '50s and performing on his own television show since 1961.

He is one of the biggest selling artists on the RCA label and his syndicated television show became the most popular show of its type—seen weekly by 45 million people in 100 markets.

Porter was raised on a Missouri farm. Times were sometimes a little tough there, and by age 14 he was helping out by working as a clerk in a local market. To take up slack time he would play guitar and sing—for customers and the owner. The owner liked his singing so much that he sponsored a 15-minute local radio show featuring Porter, "market clerk."

Porter greets the audience with his trademark "Hi."

This led to a job at KWTO in Springfield, Missouri, in 1951. A few months later, the Ozark Jubilee was born there, and soon Red Foley, who directed the casting, was teaching Porter the necessary "professional extras" that turn good entertainers into great showmen. Porter learned fast and was soon a featured performer.

Despite his lack of big time experience, RCA offered him a recording contract. In fact RCA's legendary Steve Sholes had so much faith in Porter's potential that he allowed Porter to experiment for four years until he found the right musical formula.

In 1954, his "Company's Comin'" hit the Top 10 and in 1955 "A Satisfied Mind" hit No. 1, holding there for four weeks. It was followed by a string of 30-year hits. On February 23, 1957, Porter became a member of the Grand Ole Opry.

He began his long-running syndicated country music television show in 1961. In 1967 he auditioned a young singer named Dolly Parton and she was soon his singing partner. By 1969, Porter and Dolly had won a Grammy for "Just Someone I Used To Know." Next, they were named CMA's "Duo of the Year" for three consecutive years. They had 14 Top 10 hits before their partnership ended in 1974.

Porter recorded such country standards as "Misery Loves Company," "I've Enjoyed As Much of This As I Can Stand," "The Cold, Hard Facts of Life," "The Carroll County Accident" and "Green, Green Grass of Home."

Porter Wagoner is a country star in every sense of the word—showman, television star, singer and more. His rare talent makes every person in the audience feel that Porter is performing for him or her alone. His flashy suits, sense of humor, and stage presence have made him one of the most recognized figures in country music today.

His 1992 biography *A Satisfied Mind: the Country Music Life of Porter Wagoner* takes readers behind closed doors to the real world of country music.

Billy Walker

BY THE AGE OF 15,

BILLY HAD WON HIS

FIRST SINGING CONTEST

AT KICA RADIO IN NEW

MEXICO, SINGING "I'LL

NEVER LET YOU GO,

LITTLE DARLIN.'"

At 6 feet 4 inches tall, Billy Walker is still thrilling audiences everywhere with his craft and showmanship.

It was Gene Autry who would have a lasting impact on Billy's life. At age 13, his father gave him a dime to see a Gene Autry film. From that moment on, Billy knew he was born to sing. Stardom didn't come easy for The Tall Texan. He worked plucking turkeys to earn enough money to buy his first guitar. By the age of 15, Billy had won his first singing contest at KICA Radio in New Mexico, singing "I'll Never Let You Go, Little Darlin.'" KICA Radio offered Billy his own live radio show for two years. It would mean hitchhiking 80 miles every week, but Billy had a dream.

It was the Big D Jamboree radio show in Dallas that got the ball rolling. In 1949, Hank Thompson assisted in securing Billy's first recording contract for Capitol Records. By 1952 Billy had become a mainstay on the Louisiana Hayride.

Billy welcomes his wife Bettie to the stage.

While there, Billy and Slim Whitman assisted Elvis Presley in making his first appearance on the show. Billy vividly remembers his first encounter with Elvis. "Here comes this good looking kid dressed in black pants with a pink coat and pink shoes to match," Billy says. Elvis asked if he could sing a song and "I just stood there sort of in a suspended animation until this kid goes out on stage. BANG! Instant electricity," Billy recalls. This would mark the first of many encounters with the King of Rock 'n' Roll. In 1955 Tillman Franks, Billy and Elvis joined together and toured West Texas. A young outlaw by the name of Waylon Jennings was their poster boy. Jennings assisted in promotion of the tour.

At the Ozark Jubilee, Billy learned to fine-tune his craftsmanship. It was there that he met Red Foley. A life long friendship developed. Billy was there at Red's last concert, standing in the wings as he sang his last song "Peace in the Valley." "Red taught me more about working on stage than anyone. He was a master performer," Billy commented.

After a benefit concert in Kansas City in 1963, Billy received an urgent call to return home. Hawkshaw Hawkins overheard Billy's dilemma and handed him his plane ticket. Hawkins said, "Here kid, you take this ticket and you get on that plane and you be Hawkshaw Hawkins. I'll fly home with Patsy and the others." Later, a small private plane would crash just 30 minutes from its final destination. Hawkshaw Hawkins, Randy Hughes, Cowboy Copas and Patsy Cline were dead. Billy had no idea that the plane ticket he received that day would literally save his life. For years, Billy carried a wound so deep that he couldn't speak about the loss of his friends. One day he realized the greatest tribute he could give to his friends was to sing.

Billy has had 32 Top 10 hits, over 100 chart records and numerous No. 1 hits. Willie Nelson wrote "Funny How Time Slips Away" while staying in Billy's home, and it was recently certified by BMI for a million airplays.

Billy joined the Grand Ole Opry in 1960, introduced by Ernest Tubb. "It was electric; it's not every day that you get to be a part of history," the Tall Texan remembers.

Charlie Walker

Born in Copeville, Texas, the Opry's Charlie Walker grew up on his parents' cotton farm in Nevada, Texas, about 35 miles east of Dallas. His dad was a Texas lawman and Justice of the Peace.

He started singing in high school, got a job in a Dallas honky-tonk and soon joined the "Cowboy Ramblers" for a year before Uncle Sam called.

While in Japan he brought his country music to the Japanese on the Armed Forces Radio Network from Tokyo. After the service he moved to San Antonio and became one of the country's Top 10 Country disc jockeys.

Not long thereafter, other disc jockeys were playing Charlie's records, including his first significant hit "Tell Her Lies and Feed Her Candy." He followed that with the million-seller "Pick me up on Your Way Down." In all, he's amassed 35 albums and had 47 songs on the national charts.

Charlie became an Opry member on August 17, 1967, and 14 years later the Federation of International Country Air Personalities (FICAP) inducted him into its Disc Jockey Hall of Fame.

Between tireless touring of the U.S., England, Sweden, Germany, Italy, Japan and Canada, Charlie has managed to develop a good golf game, playing in about 10 pro-celebrity golf tournaments every year. He has played the Jackie Gleason Inverarry Classic, the Sahara Invitational in Las Vegas, the Colonial Invitational, The American Cancer Classic, The Southern Open, The Greensboro Open, The Texas Open, The Westchester Classic in New York and the Atlanta L.P.G.A.

Recently Charlie decided to gather up his golf and Opry buddies and help some kids with a treatable language disorder. He established the first annual Charlie Walker Louisville Scottish Rite Celebrity Golf Scramble. All proceeds go to the Children's Language Development Center for pre-schoolers between the ages of 2 and 5 who need language therapy to enable them to attend regular school classes.

Charlie Walker: big hits, big heart and big on helping kids who are in need.

Charlie Walker welcomes his entire "Walker gang" to the Opry stage in 1995.

Steve Wariner

No one could ever make me believe I wasn't put on this Earth to write, sing, play and produce music. For that, I am eternally grateful.

—Steve Wariner

There are also a lot of Music Row insiders and country music fans who are also eternally grateful. No question about it, singer, instrumentalist, songwriter, painter, producer, showman and Opry member Steve Wariner is one heck of a talent.

And the talent has been building for years. At 9 he was playing guitar, and by age 10 he was playing bass in his father's country band. "As a young guy, all I wanted to do was play guitar," Steve says. "My mom would have to make me quit. I used to come home for lunch when I was in grade school, and as soon as I got in, I'd go straight to the bedroom and start playing the guitar. Everyday, my mom would have to yell at me, 'You better eat this sandwich and get back to school.'"

By the time he hit his teens, Steve had begun singing publicly—just because the bands he played in needed a singer. But he didn't take it seriously until Dottie West caught his show near Indianapolis. She hired him as a bass player and introduced him to the Opry. At age 17 he was playing bass for Dottie, by 22 for Bob Luman and at 24 for Chet Atkins.

Atkins signed him to RCA Records contract in 1977 and he soon had a bevy of hits, including his first No. 1 "All Roads Lead To You." Other albums and deals landed Steve in the country Top 10 with more than 30 other singles and a dozen No. 1 songs.

A life-long dream came true the night of May 11, 1996, when he joined the Grand Ole Opry with his proud parents Roy and Ilene and his wife Caryn and sons Ryan and Ross in the audience.

Around that time, Steve put performances on hold to concentrate on songwriting and came up with hits for Bryan White, fellow Opry members Clint Black and Garth Brooks and others. He's now won 11 BMI Songwriter of the Year awards. Steve also picked up Song of the Year honors from both the CMA and ACM for "Holes in the Floor of Heaven," the tune that would also win CMA Single of the Year honors and launch another professional surge of success.

Burnin' the Roadhouse Down, the album containing "Holes," went gold, as did the follow-up *Two Teardrops* which included the hit title track Steve co-wrote with Opry buddy Bill Anderson. The album received a CMA Album of the Year nomination, and the song scored a Grammy nod.

Steve's recent *Faith In You* album includes guest instrumental appearances by his sons, Ross and Ryan. "I see myself so much in both of them," Steve says, adding that he sees the same excitement in them that he had during those guitar practice sessions during his grade school lunch breaks. "I see that in these guys—that same fire."

A fire that's burned inside the singer, musician, songwriter, painter, producer, showman and Opry member for years.

Two songwriters. Grammy nominees for "Two Teardrops" Steve and Bill enjoy some time backstage.

The Whites

When The Whites sing their family harmony, it comes from lots of practice—more than 30 years of singing together around the house and performing professionally on the road. Daddy Buck and daughters Cheryl, Sharon and Rosie are all top singers and musicians individually, but when they hit the Opry stage together, they never fail to showcase the talents that have made them one of country music's all-time favorite family acts.

Father Buck was raised in Texas where he was exposed early on to Texas swing, honky-tonk and bluegrass. His fondness for cowboy star Buck Jones caused him to name himself Buck at age 10.

Buck, whose skills on the piano landed him early gigs with the Opry's Hank Snow, Ernest Tubb and others, married Pat Goza in 1951. In 1962 they moved from Texas to Arkansas where with another couple they began performing at local events as the Down Home Folks. Their children performed as the Down Home Kids.

By the mid '60s the family was well known in bluegrass circles, and when the younger Whites decided they wanted to sing professionally, the family moved to Nashville in 1971.

The next two years they performed as the Down Home Folks and recorded several bluegrass albums, mostly with other groups.

In 1973 mother Pat retired from the group, and in 1975, The Whites found themselves performing at a show in Washington, D.C., with Emmylou Harris. This association

between the two would-be Opry acts led to Sharon and Cheryl providing background vocals on Harris' 1978 *Blue Kentucky Girl* album. The Harris connection also led to a renewed friendship with Ricky Skaggs, who was playing in Emmylou's Hot Band at the time. The family had met Ricky when he played bluegrass with Ralph Stanley, and he ended up playing fiddle and singing with The Whites on a Far Eastern tour in 1979.

Two years later Ricky and Sharon married. As his solo career blossomed, so did The Whites.'

In 1982 they had their first Top 10 hit "You Put the Blue in Me." Other Top 10s followed —"Pins and Needles," "Wonder Who's Holding My Baby Tonight" and "Hanging Around."

On March 2, 1984, they joined the cast of the Grand Ole Opry. "We had been guesting on the Opry for a couple of years," remembers Sharon. "Dad had hinted to the Opry General Manager Hal Durham about making us members. Then one night Hal asked Dad if he'd like to become a permanent part of the Opry. He came to find Cheryl and me. We could tell by the look in his eyes that something wonderful had happened!" As Buck remembers, "I got mighty excited."

Cheryl adds that on the night of their induction, "the whole front section of the Opry was full of our family and friends from church. Mr. Acuff introduced us and spoke to each of us. I think all of us were speechless. He was our hero and was inducting us as members. It was foggy; like a dream."

Sharon says it's still incredible to be part of a family within the Opry family. "The Opry members love and respect each other," she says. "The fans sense this and feel that they are a part of that friendship...."

He's no White! The Whites welcome Ray Benson to the fold . . . at least for a photo.

Teddy Wilburn

Teddy Wilburn was barely 6 years old when he made his first public appearance —shivering on a Thayer street corner on Christmas Eve performing with his brothers Lester, Leslie and Doyle and sister Geraldine.

Teddy Wilburn carries on the Wilburn tradition at the Opry.

Their father got them started early. "Pop" Wilburn ordered their musical instruments from the Sears catalog, rehearsed them for over a year, constructed two hardwood floors in the backyard between two oak trees, and then invited neighbors from miles around to come to their home for backyard square dances. Everybody danced and twirled as the young Wilburns played their guitars, fiddles and mandolin.

Since their one-room schoolhouse had only a six-month term, that left the Wilburn children half a year to tour and play at local radio stations, schools, churches, and movie houses—wherever their dad, who was also their manager, agent, and PR man, could book them.

Roy Acuff caught their act in Birmingham, Alabama, told Opry management about the Wilburn kids and arranged an audition.

The Wilburn Children became regular members in 1940. However, due to the extreme young ages of the children and the show's late hours, the pressures from a child labor organization forced the Opry to terminate the children's stay after only six

months. They returned home and played small radio stations and gatherings. Sister Geraldine got married and left the act.

The four Wilburn brothers carried on and became members of the Louisiana Hayride in Shreveport, Louisiana, in 1948. They played the Hayride until the Korean Conflict took Teddy and Doyle into active service in 1951.

After their release from the Army, Teddy and Doyle went to work with Webb Pierce. By 1953, they were back on the Opry. Webb got them a recording contract with Decca Records that became a 22-year relationship.

The Wilburn Brothers' vocals became a benchmark for future country music duets and family acts, and the two had their own syndicated television show for more than 12 years. The show became a vehicle for introducing new talent, including future Opry members Loretta Lynn, the Osborne Brothers and Patty Loveless.

The Wilburn Brothers' career ended with Doyle's death on October 16, 1982. "It was like a 45-year marriage ended," Teddy said. "There was a lot of adjusting to do."

Teddy carried on as a solo act, thereby continuing the tradition of a Wilburn on the stage of the Opry—a tradition that started 60 years ago.

A TRADITION OF A

WILBURN PLAYING ON

THE STAGE OF THE

OPRY IS ONE THAT HAS

LASTED 60 YEARS.

Trisha Yearwood

"I'VE HAD THIS DREAM

FROM A TENDER AGE

. . . CALLING MY NAME

FROM THE OPRY STAGE"

Trisha Yearwood's debut single "She's In Love with the Boy" went to No. 1 and three more singles off of her debut album—"Like We Never Had a Broken Heart," "That's What I Like About You" and "The Woman Before Me" were Top 10 hits.

Not a bad start for a small town Georgia girl who moved to Nashville in 1985 to enroll in Belmont University's Music Business Program, then started singing demos while she was a Music Row intern.

She toured with Garth Brooks, won the Academy of Country Music's Top New Female Vocalist Award and the American Music Award for Top New Country Act on the strength of her multi-platinum debut.

Her second album, *Hearts in Armor*, went platinum, as well, and the project's lead single, "Wrong Side Of Memphis," included the prophetic lyric, "I've had this dream from a tender age . . . calling my name from the Opry stage."

One year later, her story was told in the 1993 book *Get Hot or Go Home: Trisha Yearwood And The Making Of A Nashville Star*, and she recorded her third album, *The Song Remembers When*, accompanied by a Disney TV special featuring her music.

Trisha celebrates her Opry induction in the Acuff Theatre.

The years that followed included more successful albums and hits such as "XXX's And OOO's" and "Believe Me Baby (I Lied)."

Then things got even busier . . . and better. "How Do I Live," the first single off her greatest hits collection *Songbook* became a monster smash and propelled the album to the top of the charts.

"That had never happened to me before," says Trisha. "Then a few months later I got to perform the song on the CMAs and then won that award (Female Vocalist of the Year), which was really a big moment for me. I grew up watching the CMA's and I had been nominated several times, but I had made my peace with not winning it."

There was more winning to be done. She also took ACM Female Vocalist honors as well as two Grammys the next year.

Trisha followed the success of *Songbook* with *Where Your Road Leads*. Though she had no way of knowing it when she titled the album, her road would lead to Grand Ole Opry membership while it was still one of country's top selling projects.

On March 13, 1999, she was introduced by Porter Wagoner as the Opry's newest member, and the packed Opry House erupted in applause when she delivered the "Wrong Side Of Memphis Line" line, "I've had this dream from a tender age . . . calling my name from the Opry stage" perhaps with more conviction than ever before.

She then said, "Roy Acuff always said, 'Sing the one that brought you,' so we're gonna sing 'She's In Love With the Boy.'" Trisha's next song was the Patsy Cline classic "Sweet Dreams." Before she accepted a standing ovation from the crowd, Trisha thanked Patsy Cline's daughter and widower for an Opry induction gift—a necklace once owned by the Opry legend.

"Having my family there, the Opry members and Patsy Cline's family there was a night I'll always cherish," Trisha says.

Induction Dates, Birthplace and More!

BILL ANDERSON
Birthplace: Columbia, South Carolina
Membership since: 1961

Q: Describe your invitation to join the Opry.

A: *Manager Ott Devine telephoned me at home while I was watching the 1961 All Star baseball game on television. I almost didn't get up to answer the phone!*

ERNIE ASHWORTH
Birthplace: Huntsville, Alabama
Membership since: 1964

Q: What has been your most memorable moment at the Grand Ole Opry?

A: *"The first time I appeared on the Opry, I was a guest with Ernest Tubb. I was very scared and I was afraid I would open my mouth to sing and nothing would come. When I sang the first word I calmed down."*

CLINT BLACK
Birthplace: Long Branch, New Jersey
Membership since: 1991

GARTH BROOKS
Birthplace: Tulsa, Oklahoma
Membership since: 1990

JIM ED BROWN
Birthplace: Sparkman, Arkansas
Membership since: 1963

Q: What do you most enjoy about playing the Opry?

A: *"Seeing all my friends."*

BILL CARLISLE
Birth place: Wakefield, Kentucky
Membership since: 1953

ROY CLARK
Birthplace: Meherrin, Virginia
Membership since: 1987

Q: Do you have a favorite song?

A: *"Yesterday When I was Young." "If I was to write a song, that's the song I'd write. Every line is so true."*

JOHN CONLEE
Birthplace: Versailles, Kentucky
Membership since: 1981

WILMA LEE COOPER
Birthplace: Valley Head, West Virginia
Membership since: 1957

SKEETER DAVIS
Birthplace: Dry Ridge, Kentucky
Membership since: 1959

DIAMOND RIO
Membership Since: 1998

LITTLE JIMMY DICKENS
Birthplace: Bolt, West Virginia
Membership since: 1948

Q: Is there an Opry performance by another artist you most vividly recall?

A: *"Hank Williams' first night on the Opry. He received six encores."*

JOE DIFFIE
Birthplace: Tulsa, Oklahoma
Membership since: 1993

Q: Is there an Opry performance by another artist you most vividly recall? Why?

A: *"Hank Locklin singing 'Danny Boy.' It tore the House down. I had cold chills."*

ROY DRUSKY
Birthplace: Atlanta, Georgia
Membership since: 1958

Q: What has been your most memorable moment as a Grand Ole Opry member?

A: *"The last night at the Ryman before we moved to Opryland."*

HOLLY DUNN
Birthplace: San Antonio, Texas
Membership since: 1989

Q: Do you have a favorite song . . . and why?

A: *"Anything The Whites sing! I just love them!"*

THE GATLIN BROTHERS

Birthplace: Seminole, Texas
Membership since: 1976

DON GIBSON

Birthplace: Shelby, North Carolina
Membership since: 1958

VINCE GILL

Birthplace: Norman, Oklahoma
Membership since: 1991

BILLY GRAMMER

Birthplace: Benton, Illinois
Membership since: 1959

Q: What has been your most memorable moment as a Grand Ole Opry member?

A: *"When the Opry moved from the Ryman to the Opry House, I was invited to give the invocation . . . and President Nixon was there."*

JACK GREENE

Birthplace: Maryville, Tennessee
Membership since: 1967

Q: What do you most enjoy about playing the Opry?

A: *"Seeing the reaction of the audience and backstage guests."*

TOM T. HALL

Birthplace: Olive Hill, Kentucky
Membership since: 1971

Q: Do you have a favorite song?

A: *"'I Love,' one I wrote myself."*

GEORGE HAMILTON IV

Birthplace: Winston-Salem, North Carolina
Membership since: 1960

Q: To what do you attribute the Opry's 75-year success?

A: *"It is the 'Mother Church,' the 'Homeplace' of country music. And there has always been a place reserved at the 'family table' for the parents and grandparents of country music as well as 'the new generation.' The Opry is a living museum of country music and undoubtedly the greatest live musical showcase in the world!"*

EMMYLOU HARRIS

Birthplace: Birmingham, Alabama
Membership since: 1992

JAN HOWARD

Birthplace: West Plains, Missouri
Membership since: 1971

Q: What do you most enjoy about playing the Opry?

A: *"Being with my extended family, the Opry artists. Most of us have been friends for many years, but I still love to watch them perform. And it still amazes me that I am one of the 'chosen few' to be a member of that great institution."*

ALAN JACKSON

Birthplace: Newnan, Georgia
Membership since: 1991

STONEWALL JACKSON

Birthplace: Tabor City, North Carolina
Membership since: 1956

JIM AND JESSE

Birthplace: Coeburn, Virginia
Membership since: 1964

GEORGE JONES

Birthplace: Saratoga, Texas
Membership since: 1969

HAL KETCHUM

Birthplace: Greenwich, New York
Membership since: 1994

Q: What would you be doing if you weren't a performer?

A: *"I'd be building cabinets and restoring old houses and writing the occasional song."*

ALISON KRAUSS

Birthplace: Champaign, Illinois
Membership since: 1993

HANK LOCKLIN

Birthplace: McLellan, Florida
Membership since: 1960

Q: What has been your most memorable moment as a Grand Ole Opry member?

A: *"Having my son, Hank Adam, sing with me on the stage at the Opry."*

CHARLIE LOUVIN
Birthplace: Sand Mountain, Alabama
Membership since: 1955

PATTY LOVELESS
Birthplace: Pikeville, Kentucky
Membership since: 1988

LORETTA LYNN
Birthplace: Butcher's Hollow, Kentucky
Membership since: 1962

BARBARA MANDRELL
Birthplace: Houston, Texas
Membership since: 1972

MARTINA McBRIDE
Birthplace: Sharon, Kansas
Membership since: 1995

Q: Is there any Opry performance by another artist you most vividly recall?

A: *"Seeing Loretta Lynn perform 'Honky Tonk Girl' onstage at the Ryman. It was like taking a step back in history and seeing the Opry as it was all those years ago. Standing there watching I was so moved and felt like I had been given a gift . . .."*

MEL McDANIEL
Birthplace: Checotah, Oklahoma
Membership since: 1986

REBA McENTIRE
Birthplace: Chockie, Oklahoma
Membership since: 1986

RONNIE MILSAP
Birthplace: Robbinsville, North Carolina
Membership since: 1976

LORRIE MORGAN
Birthplace: Hendersonville, Tennessee
Membership since: 1984

JIMMY C. NEWMAN
Birthplace: Big Mamou, Louisiana
Membership since: 1956

Q: What would you be doing if you weren't a performer?

A: *"I probably would have been a cowboy turned rancher by now."*

THE OSBORNE BROTHERS
Birthplace: Hyden, Kentucky
Members since: 1964.

146

BASHFUL BROTHER OSWALD
Birthplace: Sevier County, Tennessee
Membership since: 1995

DOLLY PARTON
Birthplace: Locust Ridge, Tennessee
Member since: 1969

JOHNNY PAYCHECK
Birthplace: Greenfield, Ohio
Membership since: 1997

STU PHILLIPS
Birthplace: Montreal, Canada
Membership since: 1967

RAY PILLOW
Birthplace: Lynchburg, Virginia
Membership since: 1966

CHARLEY PRIDE
Birthplace: Sledge, Mississippi
Membership since: 1993

JEANNE PRUETT
Birthplace: Pell City, Alabama
Membership since: 1973

Q: What has been your most memorable moment as a Grand Ole Opry member?

A: *"The many Saturday night 11:30 shows I shared the stage with my late, great friend Marty Robbins."*

DEL REEVES
Birthplace: Sparta, North Carolina
Membership since: 1966

Q: What would you be doing if you weren't a performer?

A: *"I'd have finished college and become a high school basketball coach."*

RIDERS IN THE SKY
Membership since: 1982

Q: What has been your most memorable moment as a Grand Ole Opry member?

A: *"Well obviously the night we joined was the most memorable. Ernest Tubb formally introduced us on the early show, and Roy Acuff on the late show—I think we shocked him by doing the rabbit dance instead of a dreamy classic of the West.*

— Ranger Doug of Riders In The Sky

JOHNNY RUSSELL
Birthplace: Sunflower County, Mississippi
Membership since: 1985

JEANNIE SEELY
Birthplace: Titusville, Pennsylvania
Membership since: 1967

RICKY VAN SHELTON
Birthplace: Danville, Virginia
Membership since: 1988

JEAN SHEPARD
Birthplace: Paul's Valley, Oklahoma
Membership since: 1955

RICKY SKAGGS
Birthplace: Cordell, Kentucky
Membership since: 1982

MELVIN SLOAN DANCERS
Cast members since:1952

Q: To what do you attribute the Opry's 75-year success?

A: *"The Opry's success can be equally attributed to the dedication, loyalty and desire to perform by all the past and present members of the Grand Ole Opry—whether it be singers, musicians, comedians or dancers—and the Grand Ole Opry fans that have traveled thousands of miles over the years to enjoy this country music spectacular."* — Melvin Sloan

CONNIE SMITH
Birthplace: Elkhart, Indiana
Membership since: 1965

MIKE SNIDER
Birthplace: Gleason, Tennessee
Membership since: 1990

RALPH STANLEY
Birthplace: Dickenson County, Virginia,
Membership since: 2000

MARTY STUART
Birthplace: Philadelphia, Mississippi
Membership since: 1992

RANDY TRAVIS
Birthplace: Marshville, North Carolina
Membership since: 1986

TRAVIS TRITT
Birthplace: Marietta, Georgia
Membership since: 1992

PORTER WAGONER
Birthplace: West Plains, Missouri
Membership since: 1957

BILLY WALKER
Birthplace: Ralls, Texas
Membership since: 1960

CHARLIE WALKER
Birthplace: Copeville, Texas
Membership since: 1967

STEVE WARINER
Birthplace: Noblesville, Indiana
Membership since: 1996

THE WHITES
Birthplace: Oklahoma and Texas
Membership since: 1984

Q: To what do you attribute the Opry's 75-year success?

A: *"... It found a place in the hearts and lives of people all over the country and it still does. True Opry fans are so loyal. They love you, and you love them back. In this age of technology, the Opry is still special to so many."* — Cheryl White

TEDDY WILBURN
Birthplace: Thayer, Missouri
Membership since: 1953

TRISHA YEARWOOD
Birthplace: Monticello, Georgia
Membership since: 1999

Q: To what do you attribute the Opry's 75-year success?

A: *"A strong dedication to preserving and promoting country music and its artists."*

Opry Family Ties

THE GRAND OLE OPRY. *Garth Brooks has called it the pinnacle of his success. "The Opry,"* *he said, "that **does** take the cake." Loretta Lynn refers to the first time she stepped on the Opry* *stage as "the greatest moment of my life." Patty Loveless says being an Opry member "is definitely* *a dream." And the deep-rooted feelings evoked by Brooks, Lynn and Loveless are shared by each* *of their fellow Opry cast members.*

"THERE'S

SOMETHING HERE

FOR EVERYBODY."

–Marty Stuart

Add to the picture the special guests who visit the Opry stage weekly, millions of fans world-wide and a behind-the-scenes crew that coordinates each week's shows, and one has the Grand Ole Opry, one of the most fascinating stories in the world, let alone the country music arena.

Perhaps the Opry's success lies in its broad scope and contrasts. It's the world's longest-running live radio show, yet it's also a live audience of thousands. It's country music's most famous artists on its most famous stage, and it's also friendships between artists that run much deeper than the fame they share. And while the Opry is the onstage excitement of a performance by a fan favorite, it is also a flurry of backstage activity—jam sessions, storytelling and fun.

At the heart of the Opry is its music and members—a broad scope of music by a diverse group of artists. "The Grand Ole Opry celebrates the diversity of all the musical styles under the country music umbrella," says Opry General Manager Pete Fisher. "In addition, the Opry presents the many generations of artists who have

formed country music's rich legacy and continue to forge its future course." Indeed, during any given Opry show, audiences can expect to be entertained with the best in country, bluegrass, comedy, Gospel and more by Country Music Hall of Famers, Opry cast members who helped establish the Opry as the home of country music, revered superstars and young artists just beginning to make strides in their country music careers.

Diverse and generationally separated though they may be, Opry cast members have a tie that binds, so much so that a conversation with any one member usually includes mention of their "Opry family," fellow cast members with whom they've shared years of experiences. Country Music Hall of Fame member Little Jimmy Dickens says that above the applause of the audience or the thrill of performing, what he enjoys most about playing the Opry is "being there with all my friends." Roy Clark says that "on the nights when I'm on the road, I often listen to the Opry on the radio or catch it on TV. It's almost like watching a family reunion and I'm the only one who isn't there." Clark says the Opry's 75-year success can be attributed to "the love of its members for each other and of the institution that is the Grand Ole Opry." And just as their fellow Opry members are family, the Opry, itself, is home.

Opry members also have long welcomed special guests into their home, so to speak, to share in the excitement of a live Opry performance. For every three to four cast members on any given Opry show, Fisher estimates there is a performance by a variety of potential guests. Such special guest performances serve not only to expand the variety of music the Opry offers, but also to enhance the opportunities for onstage and backstage interaction between generations of artists who might otherwise not discover each other.

As Fisher says, "The Opry show, with its presentation of the generations, challenges the younger to appreciate the older and the older to appreciate the younger. It encourages the contemporary to discover the traditional and the traditional to discover the contemporary."

Opry member Marty Stuart agrees, saying, "It's hip to come to the Opry because once you see somebody like Garth Brooks or myself or Travis Tritt that you love, you're going to discover somebody like Little Jimmy Dickens or square dancing. And there's something here for everybody."

Trisha Yearwood says that in addition to seeing the fans at the Opry, she appreciates "getting a chance to get to know and visit with country music's heroes and legends." And Martina McBride, who was inducted into the Opry by Loretta Lynn, says that watching Lynn perform is one of her all-time favorite Opry memories. "Standing there watching, I was so moved I felt

Loretta Lynn calls her Opry debut "the greatest moment of my life."

like I had been given a gift . . ." McBride said. Meanwhile, Lynn, like other Opry veterans, has enjoyed performances from special guests such as Chely Wright.

When the Opry's Jeanne Pruett thinks about the mix of generations at the Opry, her memory takes her immediately back to 1992. "Vince Gill sang 'Drifting Too Far From The Shore' at Roy Acuff's request just weeks before Mr. Roy died. That performance was a happening! It was so moving for me," she remembers. For many special guests, an Opry debut is the high point of their careers, the realization of a long-held dream. Generations of guest singers and musicians have for years said, "There's just something about the Opry" before stepping onto its

Trisha Yearwood says the magic of the Opry is twofold: the interaction with the fans and the camaraderie with "country music's heroes and legends."

It's a backstage full of music and laughs for Mike Snider and Steve Wariner.

hallowed stage for the first time. Perhaps like Patty Loveless they grew up listening to the Opry in their kitchen watching their mother mop the floor. Maybe they visited the Opry as a member of the audience and whispered to a family member that one day they'd be on the Opry stage, as did Barbara Mandrell. No matter their stories, nearly all first-time guests describe themselves as "nervous" but the experience as "wonderful."

Vince Gill remembers his first Opry visit well. "It was such a special moment for me the first time I got to play the Opry. I wanted to do it by myself . . . with just a guitar. I didn't want to share that moment with anybody 'cause I'd waited for it my whole life." Now an Opry member, Gill has played the show more than 100 times and welcomed a number of newcomers to the stage for their

debuts, including family group the Wilkinsons.

Like hundreds of Opry guests before her, Sara Evans called performing on the Opry for the first time "an absolute dream come true," adding that she made it through the performance "by pretending I was Patsy Cline."

Evans clearly isn't the only newcomer whose thoughts travel back to Opry legends such as Cline that helped establish the Opry as an American icon with a history to be treasured. That history is perhaps most strongly connected to a six-foot circle of oak wood in the center of the Opry stage on which Cline and others once stood. The circle was cut from the stage of the Opry's famous former home the Ryman Auditorium,

thereby giving newcomers and veterans alike the opportunity to sing on the same stage that has hosted Opry artists for many of the Opry's 75 years—Minnie Pearl, Uncle Dave Macon, Ernest Tubb and others. Alan Jackson says that's what makes the Opry special. "You think about people like Hank Williams, who stood on that spot of wood, and Mr. Acuff and, of course, George Jones. And just about anybody you can think of who has made country music has been on that stage. That's what makes you so nervous—to think about the historical part of the Opry and how it's played such a part in country music."

But Fisher maintains that the magic of the Opry is not found just in the circle of wood centerstage. "It's the chance for artists to meet their musical heroes backstage," he says, "to share a story with Porter

Vince Gill welcomes his friends The Wilkinsons to the Opry stage.

Wagoner, to join in on a bluegrass jam session in a dressing room, to talk with music industry friends about the latest in each other's careers. Performing at the Opry gives artists a unique perspective of their careers—the opportunity to be around the artists who have

Garth Brooks positions himself on the Opry's famed circle of wood.

forged country's legacy brings context to what they do. There's nothing like the Opry anywhere else in the world."

Just as the Opry is a show unlike any other, so, too, are the elements and people necessary to make it successful.

Terry London, president and chief executive officer, Gaylord Entertainment Company; Tim DuBois, president of Gaylord Entertainment's Creative Content Division; and Steve Buchanan, president of the Grand Ole Opry Group, work to enhance the Opry's reputation as a world-renowned entertainment showcase. The three leaders consider the Opry the crown jewel of Gaylord Entertainment Company, which is involved in

everything from tourism to songwriting, from lodging to event production, from riverboating to websites. With the Opry at the heart of Gaylord Entertainment's roots, the three keep a constant focus on maintaining the Opry's rich history while propelling the show into a new century.

With an eye on both the Opry's history and its future, Pete Fisher begins putting the pieces of Opry shows together often weeks and sometimes months before the curtain goes up each weekend. Members of the Opry cast communicate to the Opry's office personnel monthly which

Gaylord Entertainment's Terry London, Tim DuBois and Steve Buchanan work to enhance the Opry's reputation as a world-renowned entertainment showcase.

151

Patty Loveless joins her fellow cast members Wilma Lee Cooper, Marty Stuart and Jeannie Seely on stage after making a suprise Opry appearance.

weekends they're available to perform and when they're on the road. Fisher and his assistant Gina Keltner track the availability of a broad range of potential guest artists as well, communicating closely with record label personnel, artist management, agents and publicists to determine which members and guests will appear on each weekend's shows. If they're talking to a platinum-selling superstar, it might be about scheduling an Opry appearance several months down the road. If they're talking with an artist's manager, it might be about an appearance to coincide with the release of the artist's album in a few weeks. And there's always the chance that he'll talk with a member or guest about dropping in for a surprise appearance for which the Opry has become famous.

One example Fisher remembers vividly involves Patty Loveless. "It was less than an hour until show time," he recalls. A major star on the show that night had just called to cancel due to illness. I was walking down the hallway backstage thinking, 'What are we going to do?' when a voice behind me said, 'Hi, Pete.'"

Pete Fisher

The voice belonged to fan favorite Loveless, who had dropped by the Opry just to talk to old friends and enjoy the environment backstage. With little convincing from Fisher, Loveless soon surprised a packed Opry House with an on-stage duet with Porter Wagoner.

When most of the artists available for a show have been confirmed, Fisher begins to assemble the artist line-up for the weekend's shows, careful to strike the

Gina Keltner

balance for which the Opry has become famous— multi-generational, with a tip of the hat to everything under the country umbrella. As he places artists in the show, Fisher also has the opportunity to put the pieces together that will create magical moments on stage. Perhaps Bill Anderson will introduce Steve Wariner,

Martina McBride and Marty Stuart talk about the latest in their careers before Martina performs her latest hit.

with whom he wrote the chart-topper "Two Teardrops." Maybe Jeannie Seely and Lorrie Morgan will strike up a duet on Morgan's father's classic "Candy Kisses," or Vince Gill will drop in to add his vocals to a Jimmy Dickens performance. Ricky Skaggs could hang around onstage for a bluegrass collaboration with IBMA award-winners the Del McCoury Band. The possibilities are endless.

Meanwhile, the Opry's marketing and sales staff as well as its publicity firm work to make Opry fans aware of upcoming performers and shows, meeting with artist representatives to include artists in advertising as well as media and retail promotions. The staff also continuously updates the Opry's website, www.opry.com, with the latest news from the Opry and the country music industry.

And at WSM AM-650, the radio home of the Opry, staffers collect radio spots to run on Opry broadcasts, book artists for broadcasts that follow the Opry and inform listeners about upcoming Opry shows and special events. Occasionally WSM's air personalities also will treat their audiences to recorded highlights of past Opry shows.

Indeed, the Grand Ole Opry requires months of advance planning for special events and artist appearances, yet each Opry show falls into an interesting weekly timeline beginning, in actuality, with the conclusion of the previous weekend's shows. Fisher, during a Friday or Saturday night performance, might have talked with a cast member who had made arrangements with another artist to do a special performance the following weekend. Or perhaps an artist's publicist had mentioned another client who could play the Opry the following Friday. Regardless, on Monday Fisher begins to assemble all of the pieces of his "Opry puzzle" into the weekend's shows—the new country, the alternative country, Hall of Famers and newcomers, the Opry members and the special guests . . . more than 20 acts per show, in all. He also determines which artists will be featured on the portion of the Saturday night show that is televised live nationally on TNN.

By Tuesday, Fisher has completed the initial line-up for the weekend's shows and provides copies to the Opry staff for disbursement to potential Opry visitors. Without fail, the written line-up does, indeed, feature a bright mix of country styles and generations.

On this particular Tuesday, the line-up for the weekend includes Opry members such as Porter Wagoner, Bill Anderson, Jeannie Seely, Charley Pride and Steve Wariner, as well as an array of special guest artists, including Brad Paisley, the Bellamy Brothers, Pam Tillis and Clay Davidson.

As the written line-up is distributed, the staff at the Opry House begins contacting each artist on the weekend's shows to let them know of their performance nights and times. Others, meanwhile, make arrangements to promote the uniqueness of the week's shows by scheduling a radio telephone interview with one of the week's guests, confirming a television taping to be held during the week, scheduling a backstage Internet chat, servicing a release on a special upcoming appearance or any of dozens of other means employed to share the excitement of the upcoming weekend's shows.

As the week progresses, calls come into the Opry office regarding necessary changes to the line-up, additions and cancellations as well as altering performance slots to fit artists' schedules. As the changes are confirmed, they're shared with persons updating the schedule on www.opry.com, those entering information for the weekend's program and others.

Throughout the week, operators in Grand Ole Opry Group Customer

Service are selling tickets for the weekend's shows as well for performances well into the future. Within one month Customer Service representatives will speak with persons from all 50 states and at least 10 foreign countries and will process requests for tickets or information from telephone calls, mail and the Internet. Since the Opry moved to the Opry House from the Ryman, the Opry's Customer Service employees have sold more than 18 million Opry tickets—that's four times the population of the Opry's home state of Tennessee!

The Opry family truly runs deeper than just the artists who make up its cast. By Friday morning, a parade of others whose services are needed for another magical Opry show are on hand to ready for that night's performance. The Opry's stage manager runs through the line-up for the night, determining what special challenges the order of the show might present. The staff of sound, lighting and stage professionals check their equipment after its use for other Opry House activities throughout the week and prepare for another performance.

A virtual army of hosts and hostesses whose mission is to greet Opry fans as they file into the House don their customary red jackets and prepare to show fans from around the world to their seats after the Opry's big front doors open.

The arrival of the Opry's backstage desk personnel in the late afternoon signals the beginning of a whirlwind of Opry House activity that likely won't settle until the evening's shows are complete. Among the first arrivals include Opry announcers from WSM AM-650, the Opry's broadcast home. They'll take a look at the final line-up for the shows, read through the evening's radio commercials to ensure a smooth flow from performances to sponsor spots back to performances, and perhaps catch up with Opry staffers they haven't seen since the previous weekend. Security personnel make their way through the Opry's backstage area, as do persons charged with customer service, house upkeep and other areas.

The Opry's staff band as well as its back-up group, the Carol Lee Singers, also enter and ready for the night's show.

First one by one then in large groups, the evening's performers and their guests begin to check in at the Opry's backstage desk, bringing with them friends and family, band members, guitars, stage clothes and hands full of other necessary gear. Among those checking in tonight are Opry member Bill Anderson, on the verge of 40 years with the Opry, and special guest Brad Paisley, who tonight marks his 25th Opry appearance since his debut

Carol Lee Singers: (left to right) Dennis McCall, Carol Lee Cooper, Norah Lee Allen, Rod Fletcher

Grand Ole Opry Staff Band: (seated left to right) Tommy White, Hoot Hester, Kerry Marx, John Gardner (standing left to right) Tim Atwood, Billy Linneman, Spider Wilson, Jimmy Capps

on the show less than a year ago. It's obvious that the two singer/songwriter/ musicians share a respect for the Opry and each other.

"I've said in the past that the Opry is to country music what Yankee Stadium is to baseball. It is the pinnacle, the top of the mountain. And when you're in country music, it is the only place to be." Anderson says.

Much newer to the Opry stage, Paisley says he still gets excited every time he pays the Opry a visit.

The two met at the Opry just as Paisley's debut album was beginning to take off and quickly forged a unique friendship. Tonight, Paisley is one of three other artists on the segment of the Opry Anderson will host.

Checking in at the Opry's backstage desk, Anderson catches up with two friends and receives his dressing room assignment for the night. With

more than 20 acts on the show, artists share their rooms with at least one other Opry act. Anderson says that, like touring with someone, sharing a dressing room helps him get to know his fellow performers. All Opry members have a mailbox across from the backstage desk, and Anderson checks his to find several letters from fans as well as correspondence from the Opry office.

Anderson makes his way to his dressing room amid the ever-increasing sound of fiddles, guitars and other instruments being tuned in rooms along the long corridor. He checks in along the way with several friends and says hello to fans, many of

whom connect him with his own hits that brought him to the Opry almost 40 years ago, while some relate to him with songs he's recently penned for others, including Steve Wariner, Vince Gill, Mark Wills and Bryan White.

A few minutes later Paisley, who has just hit the Top 20 on the country singles chart for the third time in his young career, causes a stir with the fans assembled backstage when he makes his way toward his dressing room with his band.

Mail call: Bill Anderson talks with Brad Paisley while checking his mail at the Opry Post Office before his performance.

As Anderson, Paisley and dozens of others create a backstage bustle, so, too, do the thousands of fans assembling in the Opry House. For some, it's their first visit and the

155

Charley Pride has some backstage fun with the Opry Square Dance Band's Charlie Collins and Earl White and surprise guest Freddy Fender.

result of an hours-long drive. For others, it's one of many Opry visits they'll make this year. As show time nears and the lights dim, the crowd hushes to hear those famous words that have originated from the Opry stage and emanated over the airwaves of America's heartland for years: "And now presenting . . . the Grand Ole Opry!"

A variety of acts will take center stage in the 90 minutes before Anderson and Paisley perform. The audience delights in Porter Wagoner's signature "hello"—opening his rhinestone jacket to reveal "Hi" embroidered inside. Opry family group The Whites encourage the audience to sing and clap along on a country-gospel standard. Special

guest Kenny Chesney entertains with "the first No. 1 song I ever wrote," "You Had Me From Hello." Opry comedian Mike Snider delivers another Opry punchline: "So the guy walks in wearing a T-shirt with jumper cables around his neck. And the owner says, 'You can come in, but don't start nothin!'"

The Opry's big red curtain continues its up and down movement, revealing performances by Jeannie Seely, Charley Pride, the Bellamy Brothers with surprise guest Freddy Fender and others. Since each show offers so many acts, it's a constant flurry of activity on and off stage as acts tune up off stage, entertain centerstage, then often talk to friends in the wings after their performances. Opry group Riders In The Sky rehearses just off stage before going on to entertain with their brand of Western harmony and humor. "Always drink upstream from the herd," they advise later as the curtain goes down. "May the horse be with you."

ANNOUNCERS: Kyle Cantrell, Keith Bilbrey, Hairl Hensley, Eddie Stubbs

As the Riders exit the stage with fiddle, guitar and bass in hand, Anderson, who has made his way from his dressing room to the Opry's side stage, reviews the line-up of artists on his segment of the Opry a final time. A radio commercial fades, and Anderson's signature music kicks in. The Opry announcer proclaims, "Here With His Po' Folks band is Bill Anderson!"

"It's great to have you with us at the Grand Ole Opry!" Anderson shouts to a crowded Opry House. Are you having fun? Well, so are we!"

And they are. Anderson delivers an up-tempo song from his vast hit catalog and welcomes his first guest to the stage, Opry member Wilma Lee Cooper, whose music is preserved in the Smithsonian Institution. "They called me from Washington and said they had all of my records up there but one," Cooper tells the audience, "so I sent it to them."

"I tell people that the Opry covers the musical landscape," Anderson says following Cooper's performance. "Wilma Lee's music is rooted in the mountains of West Virginia, and this next act's songs come from the bayou country of Louisiana," he says, introducing the Opry's Jimmy C. Newman, who took Cajun music to the top of the country charts.

Between Anderson, Cooper and Newman, Paisley—standing in the wings waiting to make another Opry guest appearance—has just witnessed artists with a combined total of more

Donna Thompson, Opry payroll, greets Steve Wariner and Johnny Russell.

Little Jimmy Dickens (center) checks in at the Opry backstage desk with Jo Walker (left) and Becky Sanders (right).

Little Jimmy Dickens, Trace Adkins, Mark Wills, Clay Davidson and Opry General Manager Pete Fisher get together backstage during a typical night at the Opry.

than 100 years of experience on the Opry stage.

"It's really a pleasure to introduce this next fella," Anderson says. "I think he has one of the brightest futures in all of country music. He's had some big hit records in the past few months, and I think that's just the beginning. How about a big hand for Brad Paisley!"

The newcomer strides to centerstage as his band plays the first few chords of his hit "He Didn't Have To Be."

"Thank you all! God bless," Paisley acknowledges as he shakes Anderson's hand and makes his way off stage following his performance. Like several other artists on hand tonight, he'll complete a pre-arranged interview

with media outlets interested in his Opry appearance as well as the latest happenings in his career.

As Paisley completes his interview a few minutes later, Anderson says goodnight to everyone in the Opry

House as well as those listening on the radio. The two meet again backstage, where they talk about their plans for the weekend. Paisley will be back at the Opry the following night to appear on *Grand Ole Opry Live*, while Anderson is pulling out in a few minutes for a show in Ohio.

But he'll be back soon. As will Porter Wagoner, Jean Shepard, Vince Gill, Trisha Yearwood and the Opry's other cast members and special guests. And while the Opry changes between artists' visits, it remains a unique, vibrant, one-of-a-kind show.

Says Fisher, "The continued commitment Opry members display to regularly appear is the cornerstone of its success. The key to the Opry's longevity can be attributed to its ability to evolve with the ever-changing musical landscape of the times."

To which Anderson adds, "That's what makes it 'the Opry.'"

Jim Ed Brown (left) and Jeannie Seely (right) relax backstage with Rosa Mae Hodge and David Businda.

158

Opry Staff Members

GRAND OLE OPRY LIVE: (left to right) Curt Casassa, Roxane Russell, Rusty Wilcoxen

STAGE PRODUCTION: (left to right) Norris Kemp, Roger Young, Gary Leverett, Tim Thompson, Susan Ray, Dennis Kustes, Sue Thackrey, Tyler Bryan

OPRY MAINTENANCE: (left to right) Brad Long, Rex England, Clark Cato

HOSTESSES/MERCHANDISE/FOOD & BEVERAGE

AUDIO: (left to right seated) Vic Gabany, Beth Banks. (left to right standing) P.C. Salter, Tim Farris, Tom Hensley

SECURITY: (left to right) Fred Rose, Robbie Robinson, Johnny Nutt, Ann Trouillion, Russell Zediker, Holly Harden, with Opry Stars Jimmy C. Newman and Jan Howard

Gaylord Entertainment

Creating New Entertainment Traditions Gaylord Entertainment is a diversified entertainment company that believes in providing quality entertainment experiences that create a positive difference in people's lives. Headquartered in Nashville, Tennessee, it operates in three business groups: Hospitality and Attractions, Creative Content and Interactive Media. Among its properties are WSM Radio and Grand Ole Opry, the Opryland Hotel, the Ryman Auditorium, Acuff-Rose Music Publishing, Word Entertainment, Opryland Productions, WWTN Radio, the Wildhorse Saloon, Gaylord Sports Management, Musicforce.com, MusicCountry.com, Lightsource.com and Country Music Television International.

For more information on Gaylord Entertainment, log onto **www.gaylordentertainment.com.**

Circle Club™: *The Official Fan Club of the Grand Ole Opry*®

Country music's greatest show is celebrating its 75th anniversary and you can be part of the excitement! You're invited to join the greatest circle of fans in country music, the Circle Club.

As the Opry's official fan club, the Circle Club makes sure you're in the know about the Opry, its members and its other fans. Quarterly newsletters delivered to your door provide the latest stories and photos from backstage, recipes from Opry favorites, greetings from Opry fans across the country and much, much more!

Plus, your Circle Club membership is your exclusive pass to special fan club events and your ticket to special discounts and offers.

So take advantage of all the Circle Club has to offer! Become a member of the Opry's growing circle of fans today. Your personalized membership card, Circle Club button and a special gift will welcome you to this exclusive circle of friends right away!

Learn more about the Circle Club at www.opry.com.

Membership Dues
• $10.00 per year (U.S. and Canada; must be paid in U.S. currency)
• $12.00 per year International
• Make check or money order payable to the Circle Club.

Send to: *Circle Club, 2804 Opryland Drive, Nashville, TN 37214*
or call: *(615) 889-3060*—A customer service representative will be happy to send you an application.

THE ACUFF THEATRE

The Acuff Theatre opened in 1979, playing host to musical productions, concerts, receptions, meetings and various other events. The theatre just completed a $1 million renovation to ready itself for today's hottest touring shows. Keeping the family in mind, we are excitedly launching a full season run with lavish sets, dazzling production numbers, and wondrous vocal performances.

For tickets, schedule and information stop by the Opry Plaza Box Office or call (615) 889-3060.

Where Else But the Ryman.

The historic Ryman Auditorium, located in downtown Nashville, has thrilled audiences for more than 107 years. The Ryman has played host to everyone from Enrico Caruso to Sheryl Crow, Martha Graham to Vince Gill, John Philip Sousa to Bruce Springsteen. Guests can experience the Ryman today through self-guided tours or one of the auditorium's many musical performances.

The Ryman's self-guided tour leads you back in time through the fascinating history of one of the country's most famous landmarks. From its early days

RYMAN
AUDITORIUM.®

116 5th Avenue North
Nashville, TN 37219

as a gospel tabernacle, through its more than 30 years as home to the Grand Ole Opry, you will learn about the events and entertainers that have thrilled audiences for more than 107 years.

Today, the Ryman is known for exciting concerts, the summer Bluegrass Nights at the Ryman series, the inspirational Sam's Place concerts and musical theater productions. Musical theater productions have included the critically acclaimed *Always. . .Patsy Cline*, *Smoke on the Mountain* and the Nashville holiday tradition *A Musical Christmas Carol*.

Welcome to Opry Mills, the Newest Nashville Hit!

Be the first to experience shoppertainment first-hand at Tennessee's only shopping, entertainment and dining destination with a dynamic mix featuring over 200 retailers, unique restaurants, and high-caliber entertainment venues. Opry Mills includes the best names in manufacturer and retail outlets, off-price retailers, category-dominant stores and unique specialty stores. Themed restaurants, family entertainment, the Picnic in The Park Food Court and interactive retailers are all part of the shopping adventure. The center offers a convenient oval, racetrack layout with eye-catching main streets and courtyards, themed neighborhoods that include interactive, giant colorful video screens, musical bench, in-laid carpet musical notes, and musical whirly-gigs. Convenient entrances, information booths plus amenities like

ATMs, wheelchairs, restroom and telephone facilities are surrounded by stunning architecture—all under one air-conditioned roof. Beautiful wooden floors are divided into unique neighborhoods with coordinating store numbers to make it easy for shoppers to locate their favorite stores and activities, making Opry Mills not only an exciting shopping adventure but an experience designed with comfort and convenience in mind as well. It's all part of the Opry Mills experience. Come and explore, discover Nashville's newest hit— Opry Mills!

Wildhorse Saloon

The Wildhorse Saloon, a mecca of entertainment in America, began literally with a stampede of cattle through the streets of Music City, also known as Nashville, Tennessee. To capture the attention of Nashvillians and country music visitors, on June 1, 1994, the Wildhorse Saloon paraded a herd of cattle down Second Avenue and past the front doors of the newly opened club. Since then, the Wildhorse Saloon has continued to capture the interest of visitors with its unique attractions and one-of-a-kind capabilities.

The Wildhorse Saloon turned a three-level historic warehouse into a 66,000-square-foot award-winning restaurant, live music and dance destination. Wildhorse Saloon is simultaneously a restaurant, bar, concert site, dance venue and TV studio. Annually, more than one million music fans stampede to the Wildhorse Saloon to have a great barbeque meal, catch the hottest concerts and learn the newest dance steps.

Even though it is home to contemporary country music and dancing, the Wildhorse Saloon is rooted deep in Country traditions. Gaylord Entertainment Company, which owns the Grand Ole Opry, opened the Wildhorse Saloon in the heart of Music City near famous Music Row — home to 25 record companies.

Superstars like Brooks & Dunn, Clint Black, Alan Jackson, Marty Stuart and Tim McGraw drop into the Wildhorse Saloon and the fans come by to see them. Record labels launch new releases and concert tours

from this top-of-the-line facility, and country music fans and fan clubs alike make regular pilgrimages to this entertainment mecca.

In the six years since opening day, the Wildhorse Saloon has garnered recognition from numerous entertainment organizations including being named the Academy of Country Music "Club of the Year," as well as "Best Country/Western Club" in the Best of Nashville Reader's Poll.

GRAND OLE OPRY PLATINUM VISA® CREDIT CARD

Good news, Grand Ole Opry fans! Now you can show the world you're an Opry fan wherever you go and earn rewards at the same time. The Grand Ole Opry has its very own Platinum VISA credit card . . . thanks to a new joint venture with First USA Bank. Cardholders enjoy a low fixed percent introductory APR with no annual fee. And every time you use your Opry VISA card, you'll earn

reward points good for merchandise and more. To apply for your Opry VISA card, simply call **1-888-205-3318** or pick up an application in the lobby on your next Opry visit. And start enjoying the benefits of being a Grand Ole Opry VISA card holder . . . in addition to being a Grand Ole Opry fan.

INTRODUCING THE NEW OPRYLAND® HOTEL NASHVILLE

A lot of hotels talk about remarkable meetings, but Opryland Hotel Nashville has the action packed entertainment that makes meetings, conventions, and exhibitions extraordinary. The Land of Sweet Southern Dreams evokes the feeling of the true South as you drift along the Delta on a flatboat or gaze at magnificent waterfalls and acres of Southern gardens, all under one glass roof. As always, you'll find unsurpassed Southern hospitality and expansive meeting space, plus the finest professionals in the industry. But now, Opryland Hotel Nashville is becoming even more elegant. The Cascades lobby will be completely redesigned. Hundreds of guest rooms and hallways are being restored to new beauty, as well as the

Presidential and Governor's ballrooms. A new directional system will make way-finding a breeze. And now, the new Opry Mills℠ provides Opryland Hotel Nashville with a 1.2-million-square-foot entertainment, shopping, and dining destination. And here's another important difference. At Opryland Hotel Nashville, all this extraordinary entertainment is built-in, not added on, for a splendid meeting venue that's also a splendid value.

Opening February 2002 in Kissimmee-St. Cloud— Opryland® Hotel Florida and Spring 2003 in Grapevine—Opryland® Hotel Texas

The Opry and Ryman are just a Click away with
opry.com and ryman.com

Log on to the Ryman Auditorium and Grand Ole Opry websites, www.ryman.com and www.opry.com, respectively, to see everything they offer, from backstage photos and stories to opportunities to win trips to Nashville and these incredible venues! Opry.com includes Opry member spotlights which allow you to learn more about the artists plus log on each Friday for internet chats from backstage. The Opry line-up is posted on Opry.com each week, and Ryman.com includes a calendar of events for that historic venue. You can purchase Ryman and Opry tickets as well as merchandise on-line.

A soon-to-be launched Wildhorse Saloon site will link from the Ryman and Opry sites.

Every Friday and Saturday night, people across the nation have tuned in WSM Radio to listen to the Grand Ole Opry. Here is where the WSM Grand Ole Opry, the Mother Church of Country Music, was born 75 years ago and grew into the world's longest-running live radio show. WSM is truly America's country music station, with its legendary night-time signal, serving communities within a 750-mile radius and beyond. WSM is also the unparalleled source of news and entertainment in Nashville, one of the South's most dynamic cities. So when it comes to Nashville and country music, remember the three letters that say it all—WSM—America's country music station.

The Grand Ole Opry

THE GRAND OLE OPRY IS AS SIMPLE AS SUNSHINE. IT HAS A UNIVERSAL APPEAL BECAUSE IT IS BUILT UPON GOOD WILL, AND WITH FOLK MUSIC EXPRESSES THE HEARTBEAT OF A LARGE PERCENTAGE OF AMERICANS WHO LABOR FOR A LIVING.

– George D. Hay, founder of the Grand Ole Opry.

DeFord Bailey

In today's world of instant communication via the World Wide Web and CDs and DVDs for entertainment, it's hard to imagine a simple time when folk or Country Music had a universal appeal with Americans who labored for a living. But such a time existed just 75 years ago in this country. And 75 years ago, a simple radio show began in Nashville, Tennessee, which would evolve into a stage show and a world famous show business phenomenon.

This spontaneous, unpretentious, unabashed happening that is unique in broadcasting annals would entertain millions while adhering to Opry founder George D. Hay's first commandment: "Keep her down to earth, boys!"

This simple radio show turned phenomenon, after three-quarters of a century, is an American icon and the recognized home of Country Music. Its past is as unique as the show itself, its history as rich, colorful and distinct.

Turn back for a moment to that simple time in 1925. Calvin Coolidge was president. Television was just a dream for Scottish inventor John Logie Baird who had first transmitted human features via this new device that year. Business was good in the cities but workers in rural America weren't sharing in the wealth. They were, however, enjoying "old time tunes" thanks to a booming recording business. Thomas Alva Edison's phonograph had been around since 1877, and technical advances in the 1920s let record companies take recording equipment out of the studio into the field. Ralph Peer of Okeh Records in New York City discovered a market for genuine rural music. In January 1925 he coined the term "hillbilly music" after recording a group of musicians from North Carolina and Virginia.

The "Roaring Twenties" also saw great developments in the radio field. On November 2, 1920, radio station KDKA in East Pittsburgh, Pennsylvania, began the first regular broadcasting service by airing the returns of the Harding-Cox election. The first commercially sponsored program in

George D. Hay and Uncle Jimmy Thompson—1925

George D. Hay—The Solemn Old Judge

the United States was broadcast by New York's WEAF on May 12, 1922. By 1924, radios in the U.S. numbered over 2,500,000—up from the 5,000 receiving sets in America (most in the hands of expert technicians) just five years earlier. Nowhere was the impressive influence of radio felt more than in Nashville, Tennessee, in 1925.

That year National Life and Accident Insurance Company President C.A. Craig heeded his son Edwin's request to build a radio station to help sell insurance policies. The station's call letters were WSM, which stood for the insurance company's motto "We Shield Millions."

With the help of a young engineering student named Jack DeWitt, Edwin Craig launched his radio station on October 5, 1925. C.A. Craig dedicated the station to public service on its initial broadcast.

Present for that initial broadcast was one of America's pioneer showmen George D. Hay, a former reporter for the *Memphis Commercial Appeal*. He started his radio career after his appointment as radio editor for the newspaper. He first went on the air over the *Commercial Appeal's* station WMC in June of 1923. A year later he moved to Chicago and was appointed chief announcer of radio station WLS. Here he was voted America's most popular radio announcer in a nationwide contest conducted by *The Radio Digest*. Here, also, he originated the WLS Barn Dance, later to become known as the National Barn Dance.

A month after attending the dedicatory ceremony inaugurating WSM, Hay joined the station as its first program director. Then at 8 p.m. on November 28, 1925, he announced himself as "The Solemn Old Judge" (although he was only 30 years old) and launched the WSM Barn Dance.

Judge Hay created what was to become the Grand Ole Opry because of an experience dating back to his newspaper days seven or eight years before he joined WSM. While on assignment to cover a funeral in Mammoth Spring, Arkansas, he attended a hoedown with a group of Ozark mountaineers. Remembering the fun they had, he decided to feature rural America's music on his new show on WSM.

Legend has it that the first performer on the initial broadcast from the fifth floor WSM Studio A of the National Life offices was Uncle Jimmy Thompson, an 80-year-old fiddler who boasted that he could fiddle the "taters off the vine." He launched the show with the tune "Tennessee Wagoner," one of a thousand fiddle rounds he professed to know. His

The "Possum Hunters"—Front: Walter Leggett, Dr. Humphrey Bate, Buster Bate, Staley Walton. Standing: Oscar Stone and Aaron Albright. The first country band to play on WSM Radio

early appearance, however, was restricted to one hour.

Weekly thereafter, Judge Hay would blow his wooden steamboat whistle "Hushpuckena" and open the show with the refrain "Let 'er go, boys!"

Joining Uncle Jimmy Thompson in the early years were outstanding string bands, including Dr. Humphrey Bate's Possum Hunters, the Gully Jumpers, the Fruit Jar Drinkers and the Crook Brothers. "The Dixie Dewdrop" Uncle Dave Macon joined the cast in 1926 after several years in vaudeville and

entertained with his banjo playing until just three weeks before he died in March 1952.

Also joining the cast in 1926 was DeFord Bailey Sr., the show's first African-American member who became known nationally as "The Harmonica Wizard." Bailey's version of the "Pan American Blues" played on the harmonica preceded Judge Hay's famous ad lib that renamed the WSM Barn Dance in 1928.

WSM, a member of the National

Broadcasting Company network, also carried on Saturday nights "The Music Appreciation Hour" conducted by celebrated personality Dr. Walter Damrosch. The station followed this show with three hours of "barn dance" music.

In a 1945 pamphlet, Hay recalled how "Dr. Damrosch always signed off his concert a minute or two before eight o'clock just before we hit the air with

"The Fruit Jar Drinkers"—From left: "Grandpappy" George Wilkerson, Claude Lampley, Tommy Leffew and Howard Ragsdale

The Crook Brothers—Blythe Poteet, guitar; Kirk McGee, fiddle; Bill Etters, guitar; Herman Crook, harmonica; and Lewis Crook, banjo

Grand Ole Opry Cast—1927

"The Gully Jumpers"—From left: Bert Hutcherson, Roy Hardison, Charlie Arrington and Paul Warmack

Sam and Kirk McGee, "The Boys From Sunny Tennessee"

"Uncle Ed Poplin and His Ole Timers"—Standing left: Jack Woods and daughter, Louise, Ed Poplin. Seated: Frances Woods and Ed Poplin, Jr.

our mountain minstrels and vocal trapeze performers. We must confess that the change in pace and quality was immense. But that is part of America—fine lace and homespun cloth.

"The monitor in our Studio B was turned on, so that we would have a rough idea of the time which was fast approaching. At about five minutes before eight, your reporter called for silence in the studio. Out of the loudspeaker came the correct, but accented voice of Dr. Damrosch and his words were something like this: 'While most artists realize there is no place in the classics for realism, nevertheless I am going to break one of my rules and present a composition by a young composer from Iowa, who sent us his latest number, which depicts the onrush of a locomotive . . . .'

"After that announcement the good doctor directed his symphony orchestra through the number which carried many 'shooshes' depicting an engine trying to come to a full stop. Then he closed his program with his usual sign-off.

"Our control operator gave us the signal which indicated that we were on the air. We paid our respects to Dr. Damrosch and on the air said something like this: 'Friends, the program which has just come to a close was devoted to the classics. Dr. Damrosch told us that it was generally agreed there is no place in the classics for realism. However, from here on out for the next three hours we will present nothing but realism . . . . It will be down to earth for the 'earthy.'

'In respectful contrast to Dr. Damrosch's presentation of the number which depicts the onrush of the locomotive, we will call on one of our performers, DeFord Bailey, with harmonica, to give us the country version of his 'Pan American Blues.'

"Whereupon, DeFord Bailey, a wizard with the harmonica, played the number. At the close of it, your reporter said: 'For the past hour we have been listening to music taken largely from Grand Opera, from now on we will present 'The Grand Ole Opry!'" And the name stuck.

Soon crowds clogged the corridors of the WSM Studio to observe the performers. Edwin Craig suggested that these observers be allowed to watch in a studio so their reactions could add to the program. His suggestion led to the construction of Studio C, an acoustically designed auditorium capable of holding 500 enthusiastic fans.

Paul Howard (second from left) and his "Arkansas Cottonpickers"

The Delmore Brothers—Rabon (left) and Alton

Bill Carlisle and The Carlisles

Son Dorris and Uncle Dave Macon, "The Dixie Dewdrop"

Grand Ole Opry Cast, 1943

The Bailes Brothers

A galaxy of Opry stars take the stage.

Roy Acuff (left) and his "Crazy Tennesseans"

One of the early Grand Ole Opry Tent Shows

Bill Monroe (second from right) and one of his early "Blue Grass Boys" band

168

Charlie Walker and Carl Smith

Curly Fox and Texas Ruby before the present era of luxurious, custom-made buses

Ryman crowd, 1956

Studio C opened in February 1934 and in a few months could no longer accommodate the throngs, so the search for an appropriate home began. The first move in October 1934 was to the rented Hillsboro Theatre, a former movie house in what was then the southwest part of the city. When the audience continued to grow, Opry officials sought another hall.

The Dixie Tabernacle across the Cumberland River in East Nashville was available in 1936. Although the floor was covered with sawdust and the splintery benches were crude, the audience outgrew this location in three years.

In July 1939 the show moved to the newly constructed War Memorial Auditorium and an entrance fee of 25 cents was imposed in an effort to curb the crowd. It didn't work. The weekly crowds averaged better than 3,000. The move to the Ryman Auditorium in 1943 was a necessity.

The Ryman, which opened in 1892, had been built by riverboat captain Tom Ryman for the Reverend Sam Jones. Ryman had come to a religious tent meeting to heckle the preacher, only to stay and be converted. The Confederate Veterans reunion was scheduled in 1897, and a balcony was added for the meeting. The auditorium then could seat more than 3,000 people.

The popularity of the Opry shows was star-driven. Until 1938 the Grand Ole Opry had placed virtually all emphasis on instruments. What singers there were were subordinate to the band. All that changed when young Roy Acuff and his Smoky Mountain Boys joined the cast that year. His performance of "The Great Speckled Bird" that first night forever changed the Opry.

The show's popularity also was enhanced after it was carried on the NBC Radio Network for the first time in October 1939. Sponsored by Prince Albert Tobacco, the show featured Opry stars Uncle Dave Macon, Roy Acuff and his Smoky Mountain Boys, Little Rachel, the Weaver Brothers and Elviry and George D. Hay. The same group traveled to Hollywood the next year to make the movie *Grand Ole Opry* for Republic Pictures.

Later in October 1943, the Opry's "Prince Albert Show" segment with host Roy Acuff began airing on the national NBC Radio network on 129 stations coast-to-coast.

Throughout the 1940s Opry stars spent weekends performing on the show in Nashville and weekdays traveling throughout

169

L. to R.: Hank Williams, Milton Estes, Red Foley, Minnie Pearl, George Rosen (Radio Editor of Variety *magazine), Harry Stone, Eddy Arnold, Roy Acuff, Rod Brasfield, Lew Childre. In front: Wally Fowler*

Chet Atkins and Mother Maybelle (with guitars) and the Carter Family

the nation performing first in tent shows and later auditoriums. Artists and musicians alike crammed into automobiles and later buses as they became ambassadors for Country Music and the Grand Ole Opry.

Ernest Tubb took a group of Opry stars to New York's Carnegie Hall in 1947 and another Opry group played Constitution Hall in Washington, D.C., that same year. The Opry's first European tour in 1949 took Red Foley,

Roy Acuff, Minnie Pearl, Rod Brasfield, Little Jimmy Dickens, Hank Williams and others to U.S. military bases in England, Germany and the Azores.

In 1955 Ralston Purina began sponsoring an hour-long regional network television show from the Ryman stage which featured Opry stars. And in the early 1960s, WSM's "Friday Night Frolics," which had aired since 1948 from WSM's Studio C, moved to the Ryman to become

the Friday night Opry.

On April 6, 1968, a curfew imposed in Nashville following Martin Luther King's assassination in Memphis on April 4 forced the Opry to cancel its live performance and play a taped show on the air for the first time in its history.

By the late 1960s the Ryman Auditorium was feeling its age. The mostly wooden interior was a firetrap.

Left: Curly Fox, Zeke Clements and Roy Acuff

Curley Williams and his "Georgia Peach Pickers"

The building had no air-conditioning and only a handful of small dressing rooms for the stars to share. The Opry needed a new home and the decision was made to build it one on land some nine miles from downtown.

The new Grand Ole Opry House became the focal point of a multi-million dollar family entertainment park and music center that would be called Opryland USA.

The Opryland theme park opened first in 1972, followed by the Opry's move from downtown in March 1974. Opry stars said a tearful farewell to the old Ryman on Friday, March 15, after George Morgan sang "Candy Kisses" to close the show. After the Opry ended, Johnny Cash and June Carter Cash sang "Will The Circle Be Unbroken" on Grand Ole Gospel Time to end the final broadcast from the Ryman.

On Saturday night, March 16, after the big red curtain rose for the first time, a vintage black and white film of Roy Acuff and the Smoky Mountain Boys singing "The Wabash Cannonball" was projected on a giant white scrim. Slowly the scrim rose to reveal the King of Country Music and the entire Opry cast following him onstage performing his signature song. President Richard Nixon and First Lady Pat Nixon attended that first Opry performance in the new 4,400-seat venue and helped dedicate the Opry's new home.

To ensure that the stars didn't forget the show's most famous home and those who performed on it, a six-foot circle of dark oak flooring from the Ryman was installed in the new Opry House stage.

A year later in March the Cumberland River flooded Opryland theme park's parking lot, forcing the Opry to celebrate the Opry House's first anniversary in the Municipal Auditorium downtown. More than 7,000 attended the broadcast—the largest Opry audience ever.

The 1970s also saw the simple little radio show televised live for the first

Porter Wagoner

Cousin Jody (left) with Lonzo and Oscar

Hank Williams, a Country Music Legend

Patsy Cline and Ernest Tubb

Cowboy Copas and George Morgan

Gentlemen Jim Reeves, Jack DeWitt and Del Wood

The hilarious comedy team of Minnie Pearl and Rod Brasfield

time ever. The national PBS Television Network televised the show on March 4, 1978, and annually through 1981. Then in April 1985, a half-hour segment of the Opry began airing each Saturday night on TNN as *Grand Ole Opry Live. Opry Backstage*, a live 30-minute series that airs before *Opry Live* on TNN, began broadcasting in 1987.

The Opry wrote another chapter in its history book on July 8, 1990,

with a special performance for President George Bush and the heads of state attending the Economic Summit of Industrialized Nations in Houston, Texas. Opry members Roy Acuff, Larry Gatlin and the Gatlin Brothers (Steve and Rudy), Loretta Lynn, Bill Monroe and Minnie Pearl plus special guest Charley Pride performed a typical Opry show, complete with band changes and announcer breaks delivered by Opry announcers Grant Turner and Keith

Bilbrey, in the 5,000-seat Astroarena.

The following year, True Value Hardware and Home Centers sponsored a 10-city Grand Ole Opry Tour to celebrate the Opry's 65th anniversary. The tour opened April 4, 1991, in Detroit, Michigan, (with a taped message from President Bush) and closed June 15 in Joliet, Illinois. Stops in between were in Mobile, Alabama, Jacksonville, Florida, Pittsburgh, Pennsylvania,

Charlotte, North Carolina, Little Rock, Arkansas, Kansas City, Missouri, Richmond, Virginia, and Columbus, Ohio.

The Joliet show, sadly, was the last public performance for Opry legend Minnie Pearl. The Queen of Country Comedy suffered a stoke just days after returning from Illinois. She died in March 1996. That same year in September another Opry legend Bill Monroe passed away. The Opry's patriarch Roy Acuff, who died in November 1992, preceded them in death. Fellow 50-year Opry member Grandpa Jones died in February 1998.

Clearly the Opry was losing its legends. Thankfully, a move in the 1980s by Opry management ensured the show's future. A new generation of Opry stars joined the roster beginning with the induction of Ricky Skaggs, Lorrie Morgan, Reba McEntire, Ricky Van Shelton, Patty Loveless and Holly Dunn in the '80s.

By the end of the 1990s, country superstars—including Garth Brooks, Clint Black, Alan Jackson, Vince Gill, Steve Wariner, Diamond Rio and Trisha Yearwood—would call the Opry home.

The Opry surprised Yearwood with her invitation to join the cast when the show was broadcast for the first time in 25 years from the Ryman Auditorium on January 15-16, 1999. In January 2000 the Opry returned to the Ryman for a special month-long run. A new generation of Opry stars joined the legends and veterans to usher this simple radio show into the next century and beyond.

Today, 75 years after its founding, the Grand Ole Opry is still entertainment, pageantry, vaudeville and the music of all the people packaged into one presentation. The music is genuine, down-to-earth, and honest. It is realism. As Judge Hay explained once, "The principal appeal of the Opry is a homey one. It sends forth the aroma of bacon and eggs frying on the kitchen stove on a bright spring morning. That aroma is welcomed all the way from Maine to California."

The only difference in Judge Hay's WSM Barn Dance seven decades later is that today's Opry fans are probably microwaving their bacon and eggs.

The Louvin Brothers—Charlie (left) and Ira (right) with Faron Young

Edwin W. Craig, Dizzy Dean and Stringbean

Earl Scruggs and Lester Flatt

Taking Care of Business

The success of WSM Radio and the Grand Ole Opry put the music in Music City.

For more than three-quarters of a century, the Opry and WSM Radio have directly influenced Nashville's economic and physical growth. Without their dedication to country music and its nurturing of talent, it is doubtful the industry would have centered in Nashville.

"Without the Opry, I don't believe we could have had a Music City USA," WSM Radio Executive E.W. Craig has said. "It came to be the dream of every folk musician to be on the Opry. It was only a matter of time until 'cowboy laments' and other new songs were written for Opry performers. They became popular, but it meant a complete shift away from folk music. These new songs were popularized on the Opry, then played on the jukeboxes around the country. They gave rise to a whole new gamut of country western music with Nashville and the Opry being the musical backbone."

The Opry boosted Nashville as a destination for tourists as well.

From every state in the Union and many foreign countries, 700,000 Opry fans annually travel an average of 1,000 miles round-trip to see the Friday and Saturday performances. An estimated seven to eight million more fans see Opry stars who journey three million miles a year to make appearances in fans' hometowns.

Today the Nashville Area Chamber of Commerce proclaims that the city's music industry, an offshoot of the Opry, is a billion-dollar a year business.

The statistics are impressive indeed. Nashvillians are employed by recording studios, talent agencies, trade papers, recording companies and performing rights organizations. Through the Opry, WSM has created a musical family that has in turn made Nashville "Music City USA." In fact, David Cobb, retired WSM personality, is responsible for dubbing the town "Music City" many years ago.

The first recording studio, Castle, was put together by three former WSM engineers Aaron Shelton, George Reynolds and Carl Jenkins.

And the man generally considered the father of Music Row's recording industry was Owen Bradley, former musical director of WSM.

Opry legend Roy Acuff and Fred Rose both worked at WSM. The two teamed to form Acuff-Rose, Nashville's first music publishing company. Jack Stapp, program director and producer of

Two members of the Country Music Hall of Fame, Grant Turner and Tex Ritter, answer a listener's call at the WSM Radio studio.

WSM Tower

A Cast of Thousands

the old Opry network shows for NBC, formed Tree Publishing Company, and BMI Head Frances Preston once worked at WSM in the promotion department. Other WSM alumni include Chet Atkins, Francis Craig, Ernie Ford, Phil Harris, Kitty Kallen, Anita Kerr, Snooky Lanson, James Melton and Dinah Shore.

The body and soul of music is the musician and WSM and the Grand Ole Opry have been patrons of live music for more than seven decades. In addition to artists who have been Opry members for 20, 30, 40 and even 50 years, hundreds of stars and thousands of "sidemen" have performed on the Opry. WSM also employed dozens of staff musicians in the pop field and later the company gave America its first FM radio station and Nashville its first television station.

WSM and the Opry's greatest influence on the growth and economy of Nashville was the construction of a multi-million dollar family entertainment park and music center that spawned the Opryland USA entertainment complex—now home to the Grand Ole Opry, the Opryland Hotel and Opry Mills.

And the rest, as they say, is history.

Throughout its 75-year history, the Grand Ole Opry cast list could be deemed a virtual "who's who" of Country Music.

Stars have joined and left its ranks for various reasons—career, health or economic, to name a few—during the seven decades of the show. Literally hundreds of artists have called the Opry home at one time or another.

Currently, the cast includes 70 members who are honored to add their names to the selective list of stars who are members of the Grand Ole Opry family.

Here is a list by decades of just some of the stars whose names have appeared on the Opry roster during the past 75 years.

1920s
Uncle Jimmy Thompson, DeFord Bailey, the Possum Hunters, the Gully Jumpers, the Crook Brothers, the Fruit Jar Drinkers, the Binkley Brothers (Gale and Amos) and their Clodhoppers, Uncle Ed Poplin and his Ole Timers, Uncle Dave Macon, Uncle Joe Mangrum and Fred Schriver

1930s
Sam and Kirk McGee, Arthur Smith and His Dixieliners, Asher and Little Jimmy Sizemore, Robert Lunn, the Vagabonds, Leroy "Lasses" White, Jamup and Honey, Sarie and Sally, Zeke Clements and the Bronco Busters, Jack Shook and His Missouri Mountaineers (Nap Bastien and Dee Simmons), the Delmore Brothers (Rabon and Alton), Curly Fox and Texas Ruby, PeeWee King and the Golden West Cowboys, Roy Acuff and the Smoky Mountain Boys, Little Rachel, Bill Monroe and the Blue Grass Boys

Whitey Ford, "The Duke of Paducah"

1940s
Paul Howard and the Arkansas Cotton Pickers, Minnie Pearl, Ernest Tubb, Bradley Kincaid, Whitey Ford (the Duke of Paducah), the Bailes Brothers (John and Walter), Rod Brasfield, Lew Childre, Red Foley, Eddy Arnold, Lonzo and Oscar, Grandpa Jones, Cowboy Copas, Stringbean (Dave Akeman), George Morgan, Little Jimmy Dickens, Hank Williams, Cousin Jody, Johnny and Jack

The Everly Brothers—Don & Phil

Edwin Craig

Jan Howard and Bill Anderson

Left to right: Johnny Wright, Carl Smith, Tex Ritter, Webb Pierce, Smilin' Eddie Hill and Jack Anglin

Tex Ritter and Webb Pierce backstage

Johnny Cash

Eddie Hill and Hank Snow

Hawkshaw Hawkins

Kitty Wells

1950s

Hank Snow, Mother Maybelle Carter and the Carter Sisters, Faron Young, Martha Carson, the Carlisles, Kitty Wells, Webb Pierce, Carl Smith, Lester Flatt and Earl Scruggs, Ray Price, Ferlin Husky, the Jordanaires, Marty Robbins, Don Gibson, The Stoney Mountain Cloggers, the Ralph Sloan Dancers, Billy Grammer, the Louvin Brothers (Charlie and Ira), Jean Shepard, Justin Tubb, The Willis Brothers (Guy, Skeeter and Vic), Lefty Frizzell, Margie Bowes, Hawkshaw Hawkins, Del Wood, Stonewall Jackson, the Wilburn Brothers (Teddy and Doyle), Rusty and Doug Kershaw, Melba Montgomery, Jim Reeves, Jimmy C. Newman, Roy Drusky, Johnny Cash, Archie Campbell, The Everly Brothers, Wilma Lee and Stoney Cooper, Porter Wagoner, Skeeter Davis

1960s

George Hamilton IV, Patsy Cline, Bill Anderson, Hank Locklin, Bobby Lord, Marion Worth, Leroy Van Dyke, Dottie West, Tex Ritter, Bobby Bare, Connie Smith, Bob Luman, Billy Walker, Sonny James, Carl and Pearl Butler, Ernie Ashworth, Loretta Lynn, The Osborne Brothers, Jim and Jesse, The Glaser Brothers (Tompall, Jim and Chuck), Jim Ed, Maxine and Bonnie Brown, Jack Greene, Dolly Parton, Del Reeves, George Jones, Mel Tillis, Jeannie Seely, Stu Phillips, Charlie Walker, The Four Guys, Ray Pillow, Willie Nelson, Norma Jean

1970s

Jerry Clower, Larry Gatlin and the Gatlin Brothers (Steve and Rudy), Tammy Wynette, Tom T. Hall, David Houston, Jan Howard, Barbara Mandrell, Jeanne Pruett, Ronnie Milsap

1980s

Boxcar Willie, John Conlee, Ricky Skaggs, Riders In The Sky, The Whites (Buck, Sharon and Cheryl), Lorrie Morgan, Johnny Russell, Reba McEntire, Mel McDaniel, Randy Travis, Roy Clark, Ricky Van Shelton, Patty Loveless, Holly Dunn

1990s

Mike Snider, Garth Brooks, Clint Black, Alan Jackson, Vince Gill, Emmylou Harris, Travis Tritt, Marty Stuart, Charley Pride, Alison Krauss, Joe Diffie, Hal Ketchum, Brother Oswald, Martina McBride, Steve Wariner, Johnny PayCheck, Diamond Rio, Trisha Yearwood

2000

Ralph Stanley

Stoney & Wilma Lee Cooper

March 16, 1974, President and Mrs. Richard Nixon attend the premiere performance at the new Opry House. Here Roy Acuff tries to help President Nixon learn the art of the Yo Yo. Since that historic initial show, the Opry House has welcomed government officials and celebrities from all walks of life. And in June 1976, for the first time in its history, Ambassadors to the United Nations assembled away from their New York headquarters and visited the Grand Ole Opry for a special performance.

Ferlin Husky and Vito Pellettieri, who became the Opry's Stage Manager in 1934

GAYLORD ENTERTAINMENT IS ONE OF THE FEW COMPANIES THAT CAN SAY, "IT ALL STARTED IN A SMALL RADIO STATION IN NASHVILLE, TENNESSEE, IN 1925."

ALTHOUGH THE NAME GAYLORD ENTERTAINMENT COMPANY FIRST APPEARED ON THE NEW YORK STOCK EXCHANGE IN1991, THIS COMPANY'S ROOTS GO BACK 75 YEARS.

October 5, 1925

The National Life and Accident Insurance Company's new radio station WSM goes on the air. WSM began as a 1,000-watt station—one of only two in the entire South with that much power, which was twice as strong as 85 percent of all stations in the United States. It would increase to 5,000 watts in 1927.

November 28, 1925

The "WSM Barn Dance" (forerunner of the Grand Ole Opry) is launched and becomes the Grand Ole Opry on December 8, 1928.

1932

WSM is awarded a clear channel at 650 kilocycles and receives approval from the Federal Radio Commission to increase its power from 5,000 to 50,000 watts.

1941

WSM gives America its first commercial frequency modulation (FM) radio station—W47NV (forerunner of WSM-FM, which makes its debut in 1968).

September 30, 1950

WSM brings Nashville its first television station WSM-TV (an NBC affiliate), after building a series of five microwave relay stations between Nashville and Louisville, Kentucky. The station also is the first to bring color programming to Nashville.

May 27, 1972

The 400-acre Opryland theme park opens and entertains more than 54 million guests before closing 26 seasons later on December 31, 1997.

March 16, 1974

The Grand Ole Opry moves into the 4,400-seat Grand Ole Opry House at Opryland USA.

1974

Opryland Productions, a television and commercial production operation, goes into business in the Grand Ole Opry House. Two years later it receives three Emmy Awards for videotape editing for ABC-TV's coverage of the 1976 Montreal Olympics.

November 27, 1977

The Opryland Hotel, Tennessee's largest convention hotel property, opens with 600 rooms. It adds 467 rooms and the two-acre Conservatory in 1983 and another 824 rooms and the two-acre Cascades in 1988.

March 11, 1981

The NLT Corp., parent company of WSM Inc., announces plans for the sale of WSM-TV to make way for WSM's entry into satellite and cable television programming.

March 7, 1983

The Nashville Network (TNN) launches. Its initial subscriber base of close to seven million is a cable television record and in less than five years totals more than 50 million.

September 1, 1983

The American General Corporation, which had acquired National Life in 1982, finalizes the sale of the Opryland properties to the Gaylord Broadcasting Company of Dallas, a subsidiary of the Oklahoma Publishing Company, owned by Edward L. Gaylord of Oklahoma City. Opryland USA Inc. is created as a result of the sale.

July 15, 1984

Gaylord Syndicom, responsible for the long-running, highly successful syndicated country music show *Hee Haw*, is created as a division of Opryland USA Inc. to develop television shows for broadcast syndication.

June 10, 1985
Opryland USA Inc. completes the purchase of the Acuff-Rose group of publishing companies. Nashville's first music publishing company was founded by Opry star Roy Acuff and songwriter/entertainer Fred Rose in 1942 and its catalog of copyrighted songs includes country and pop standards by songwriters such as Hank Williams, Pee Wee King, Dallas Frazier, Roy Orbison and the Everly Brothers.

July 2, 1985
The General Jackson, a $12 million paddlewheel showboat, which can carry 1,200 passengers, is christened by Mrs. Thelma Gaylord in ceremonies at Nashville's Riverfront Park. Operation on the Cumberland River begins July 3. The company has since added the Music City Queen paddlewheeler and Opryland River Taxis to its fleet.

September 1990
Opryland Hotel's Springhouse Golf Club (an 18-hole golf course and clubhouse) opens.

January 1991
Opryland USA Inc. and Group W Satellite Communications purchase Country Music Television (CMT)

October 24, 1991
Gaylord Entertainment Company, listed on the New York Stock Exchange as GET, offers its stock to the general public.

October 19, 1992
CMT Europe is launched, broadcasting country music videos via satellite from Nashville to Western Europe.

November 15, 1992
WSM's Grand Ole Opry is inducted into the Museum of Broadcast Communications' Radio Hall of Fame.

June 1, 1994
The Wildhorse Saloon country music dance club opens to the public downtown. In 1998 the company opens another Wildhorse Saloon in Orlando, Florida.

June 6, 1994
The Ryman Auditorium reopens to the public as a performance hall and museum.

July 25, 1995
WWTN-FM Radio, a Nashville news/talk/sports format station, joins the family.

June 1, 1996
The Opryland Hotel Convention Center completes its $175 million expansion. The largest hotel/convention center under one roof anywhere in the world now boasts 2,884 rooms, 600,000 feet of exhibit and meeting space and the Delta, a 4.5-acre garden area.

Grandpa Jones, David Houston and Ralph Sloan

An historic occasion, celebrating the purchase of Opryland USA Inc. by Gaylord Broadcasting, July 1, 1983. Making the announcement on the Opry stage are (left to right) Sam Lovullo, producer of Hee Haw, E. W. "Bud" Wendell, Mrs. Thelma Gaylord, Minnie Pearl, Edward L. Gaylord, chairman of Gaylord Broadcasting, and Roy Acuff.

Bashful Brother Oswald and Boxcar Willie

179

January 7, 1997
Gaylord Entertainment acquires Word Records and Music, a contemporary Christian music company.

February 10, 1997
Gaylord Entertainment announces the sale of its cable networks, TNN and CMT to Westinghouse/CBS. The merger transaction with CBS is completed on October 1.

June 17, 1997
The National Hockey League announces the addition of four teams, including one in Nashville. Gaylord Entertainment is a minority owner of the Nashville Predators.

1998
Gaylord Entertainment forms the Opryland Lodging Group to develop convention hotels in other cities. Its first projects are the 1,400-room Opryland Hotel Florida, (opening 2002), the 1,500-room Opryland Hotel Texas in Grapevine near Dallas-Fort Worth (opening 2003) and the 2,000-room Opryland Hotel Potomac in Prince George's County, Maryland, (opening 2004). Gaylord Entertainment also acquires Pandora Films and Cornerstone Sports, which it renames Gaylord Sports Management.

1999
Gaylord Entertainment adds Gaylord Event Television, Corporate Magic, and Gaylord Digital with investments in CountryCool.com, Soundmarket.net, Musicforce.com, Lightsource.com and Songs.com.

March 3, 2000
Radio & Records names WSM-AM Country Radio Station of the Century.

April 2000
WordOnline Records.com, the first full-service, Internet-based, cyber-label in the contemporary Christian music industry, is launched.

May 11, 2000
Opry Mills, a 1.2 million square-foot entertainment and shopping destination built adjacent to the Grand Ole Opry House and the Opryland Hotel Convention Center, opens. The $200 million year-round attraction is a project of the Mills Corporation. Gaylord Entertainment holds a one-third interest in the partnership.

June 10, 2000
The Grand Ole Opry launches a 14-month celebration of its 75th anniversary.

Young Doyle Wilburn and Marty Robbins (right) at the WSM Radio studio with D.J. T. Tommy Cutrer (center)

March 4, 1978. For the first time in its colorful history, the Grand Ole Opry is televised live over the national PBS Television Network.

The curtain rises—followed by a fast fiddle tune, an enthusiastic crowd, intricate square dancing—and the Grand Ole Opry eagerly begins another historic evening.